GROWING
ORCHIDS

Series Editor James B. Watson

2002 *Revised Edition*

American Orchid Society
Delray Beach, Florida

American Orchid Society

CONTENTS

59

67

71

82

Growing Orchids @ 2002 American Orchid Society, 16700 AOS Lane, Delray Beach, Florida 33446-4351 (telephone 561-404-2000; fax 561-404-2100; e-mail TheAOS@aos.org; Web Site orchidweb.org). Library of Congress Catalog Card Number 2001 132031. ISBN 0-923096-05-1.

The opinion and recommendations that appear in this publication regarding the selection and use of specific plant-care products, including but not limited to pesticides, fungicides and herbicides, are those of the individual authors, and not those of the America Orchid Society, which neither adopts nor endorses such opinions and recommendations and disclaims all responsibility for them. When selecting and using such products, readers should seek and obtain the advice of the manufacturer and of responsible government agencies. 01.10.15M

INTRODUCTION

THE LARGEST FAMILY OF FLOWering plants? Orchids. The largest specialty horticulture group? The American Orchid Society (AOS). Welcome to the exotic, seductive world of orchids.

No other group of plants commands as much fanatic devotion as orchids. Your first visit to an orchid show, or an orchid nursery, or just to the corner nursery with its display of flowering orchid pot plants, will show you why. The array of colors, forms, textures and perfumes available in orchid flowers is second to none. And, many are relatively easy to grow under home conditions, or on your sun porch or patio. Even if you choose not to actually grow orchids, they are among the most exotic and cost-effective of all flowering plants for home decoration. You can expect weeks of glory for the same price you might pay for an arrangement lasting only days. But be forewarned, most people are quickly seduced by the exotic appeal of the orchid and become lifetime advocates of the group. In other words, they become orchid hobbyists.

Beauty alone cannot explain the intense fascination with which orchids are regarded. No other flower has been the object of such intense interest or the subject of considerable mythology, much of it fanciful in the extreme.

Rex Stout's great fictional detective Nero Wolfe raised orchids in the rooftop greenhouse of his Manhattan brownstone — and woe to the client who insisted on disturbing his precious four hours at the potting bench.

Basil St. John, mysterious husband of comic-strip reporter Brenda Starr, required a special serum to live — a serum extracted from the equally mysterious (and completely fictitious) black orchid.

Author H.G. Wells, pioneer of the science fiction novel, wrote of deadly carnivorous orchids that hungered for humans. In other eras, orchids were widely believed to instill virility in those who consumed their tubers.

The myths about orchids arose because of their great variety and complexity. More than 25,000 species are known to exist, and new species are discovered on a regular basis. Present-day hybrids are cultivated in greenhouses, on windowsills and under lights worldwide. Orchids are native to the tropics, certainly, but they also grow wild in North America and Europe; some species of orchid is native to every state in the United States, including Alaska. Yes, there are tropical orchids, but there are also arctic orchids.

In this book, we hope to dispel one final myth about orchids — that they are difficult to grow. Orchids are tough plants that thrive in a variety of conditions. Like any plant (or animal), orchids require care. But they respond favorably, even eagerly, to proper treatment, and reward their caretakers by blooming luxuriantly for, at times, weeks and months on end.

There is much to learn about orchids, but much is known already. Herein, the wisdom and experience of some of the world's leading authorities is distilled for your benefit. Think of *Growing Orchids* as a helpful companion, always available for consultation. You may also find it beneficial to join one of the many local AOS Affiliated Societies (see page 100), where you can learn more about orchids, and visit our Web site, orchidweb.org.

So welcome, again, to the exotic world of orchids. Growing orchids, you will find, is an intense affliction. It is never fatal, however, and it is almost entirely pleasant and immensely rewarding.

Lee S. Cooke
American Orchid Society
Executive Director

BACKGROUND

The Orchid Family

■

Intergeneric Hybrids

■

Orchid Names

■

The Benefits of Judging Orchids

Cymbidium Red Imp 'Red Tower' (Alderman x *pumilum*) flowers from Christmas through mid-winter, bearing fragrant flowers on arching inflorescences. Unlike many cymbidiums, it does not require a long cool period to initiate buds. Grower: Charles Marden Fitch.

The Orchid Family

Edited By Gustavo A. Romero-González, PhD

THE ORCHIDACEAE IS AMONG THE largest families of flowering plants. Botanists who study these plants estimate there are from 17,000 to 35,000 species; well-documented reports estimate there are around 25,000 species. Although the largest number of genera and species may be attributed to the sunflower family (Compositae), few would doubt the pre-eminence of the Orchidaceae in beauty and in the complexity of its flowers and pollination mechanisms.

Orchids are found in many habitats. Exploring for orchids in the New World Tropics might lead one to a montane cloud forest in Monteverde, Costa Rica (opposite), which is home to a rich variety of orchids. Many tropical orchids are epiphytes, or air-plants, including *Masdevallia hirtzii* (above), which grows on the limbs of trees. It is native to the misty cloud forests of the Cordillera del Condor in southeastern Ecuador. In temperate areas, most orchids are terrestrial, including this North American *Cypripedium* x*columbianum*, which is rooted at the edge of a marsh (right).

Orchids exhibit two basic growth habits: monopodial and sympodial. *Vanda* Hilo Blue 'William Look', CCM-AM/AOS (Bill Sutton x *coerulea*), illustrates the monopodial habit.

Cattleya Mandu 'Cheryl Lynn', CCM-HCC/AOS (Coquina x *amethystoglossa*), shows the sympodial habit of growth. Grower: Gold Country Orchids.

The orchids also excel in colors, fragrances and size, ranging from microscopic plants (*Platystele*) to long vines (*Vanilla*) to gigantic plants (*Grammatophyllum*). Orchids grow in all terrestrial ecosystems, except in the North and South Poles, but their greatest diversity is found in the tropics. Orchids occur on the ground (terrestrials), on rocks (lithophytes) and on trees (epiphytes); there are even well-documented cases of fully subterranean orchids in Australia. Terrestrial orchids predominate in temperate habitats, epiphytes in tropical habitats.

Orchids may be divided into two fundamental types based on growth habit. Sympodial orchids, such as cattleyas and paphiopedilums, are characterized by individual shoots with limited growth. Creeping stems called rhizomes are made of basal portions of successive shoots. Buds give rise to new shoots, each developing to maturity and flowering. Stems of many sympodial orchids develop into storage organs (pseudobulbs), which vary tremen-

dously in size and shape. Shoots of monopodial orchids, on the other hand, have unlimited growth, each continuing to produce leaves from the stem apex and inflorescences from between the leaves. Vandas and phalaenopsis are monopodial in habit.

Leaves may be tough and leathery (coriaceous) or thin and flexible (membranaceous), can have a single fold at the midline (conduplicate), or be pleated, with several prominent veins (plicate), round in cross-section (terete), or laterally flattened (equitant). With few exceptions (*Epistephium*), the major veins of orchid leaves are more-or-less parallel, as in most other monocotyledons. Most orchids are not grown for their foliage, but the mottled leaves of some paphiopedilums and the iridescent leaves of the jewel orchids (*Ludisia, Anoectochilus*) are attractive.

Roots of epiphytic orchids, and even some terrestrials, have a characteristic epidermis (velamen), which is specialized for protection of interior tissues from water

STEPHEN INGRAM

Costa Rica is one of the most popular destinations for orchidists who wish to view orchids in their native habitats. The country's excellent national reserve system protects dozens of species, which occupy a diversity of habitats. In Braulio Carrillo National Park *Miltoniopsis warscewiczii* may be seen growing on moss-covered limbs.

loss and, very likely, for water and mineral uptake also.

Flowers of all orchids are constructed on a certain basic formula. There is an outer whorl of three generally similar segments called sepals. In some genera, such as *Paphiopedilum*, the two lateral sepals are fused into one unit, then called the synsepal. Within the sepals is another whorl of three segments called petals. The median petal is almost always differentiated from the other two by size, color and/or complexity and is called the labellum or lip. Making up the center of the flowers is the column, representing the fusing of elements of the stamens and pistil. Unimaginable variation of the basic floral plan among the thousands of species and their hybrids allows for a never-ending fascination with the orchid family or Orchidaceae.

(*Gustavo A. Romero-González, PhD, is keeper at the Oakes Ames Orchid Herbarium, Harvard University.*)

The Orchid Flower

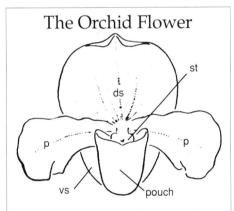

UNDERSTANDING THE structure of orchid flowers permits a greater appreciation of their beauty, as well as an ability to convey specific details to fellow hobbyists. Here, a *Paphiopedilum* flower illustrates the basic parts. Key: ds = dorsal sepal; p = petal; st = staminode; vs = ventral sepal (synsepal). In most orchid flowers, there are three sepals in an outer whorl. However, in *Paphiopedilum* the lateral sepals are fused into one unit, then called the synsepal.

Intergeneric Hybrids

By Ned Nash

ONE UNIQUE FEATURE OF ORCHIDS is the viability of hybrids not only between species, but between related genera. Traditionally, one of the definitions of a species is that it is reproductively isolated from its closest relatives. For example, real human-chimp hybrids are not seen. Because the orchid family is so recently evolved, physiological barriers to interspecific (between species) and intergeneric (between genera) hybrids are not well developed; seasonal, geographic and pollinator barriers suffice.

Perhaps as much because early orchid growers had not learned what constituted a valid species or genus as from a spirit of adventure, it was seen more than 100 years ago that hybridizing within the orchid family did not follow the same rules as in other groups of flowering plants.

By the beginning of this century, nomenclatural rules had developed into the uniform naming of intergeneric hybrids. Hybrids between two genera are always a contraction of the two generic names, such as *Brassocattleya* (*Brassavola* x *Cattleya*), *Odontonia* (*Odontoglossum* x *Miltonia*) and *Ascocenda* (*Ascocentrum* x *Vanda*). Usually, hybrids with three genera in the background are also contractions. *Brassolaeliocattleya* (*Brassavola* x *Laelia* x *Cattleya*) and *Vascostylis* (*Vanda* x *Ascocentrum* x *Rhynchostylis*) are a few of these. However, hybrid genera with three genera in their background can also end with -ara, which is used for hybrid genera of four or more genera. The genus name is derived from the originator's name (or choice of name) with an -ara suffix — *Potinara* (*Brassavola* x *Laelia* x *Cattleya* x *Sophronitis*) or *Vuylstekeara* (*Miltonia* x *Odontoglossum* x *Cochlioda*).

Unfortunately, the generic composition of a hybrid genus cannot always give all the cultural hints that a beginner might want. A classic example is the myth that all *Cattleya* hybrids containing *Laelia* are more temperature tolerant than pure-bred cattleyas. The type thought of by most in this myth have only *Laelia purpurata* in their background, and then only several generations back. Another example might be that all ascocendas are compact growing because of the *Ascocentrum* background. Again, this influence may be so far back that the plants themselves are indistinguishable from a regular standard *Vanda*. These are sometimes known as Vandacendas.

(Ned Nash is director of conservation at the American Orchid Society.)

Some Intergeneric Orchid Hybrid Genera

Genus	Abbreviation	Parentage
Aeridovanda	Ardv.	Aerides x Vanda
Brassolaeliocattleya	Blc.	Brassavola x Cattleya x Laelia
Christieara	Chtra.	Aerides x Ascocentrum x Vanda
Devereuxara	Dvra.	Ascocentrum x Phalaenopsis x Vanda
Dresslerara	Dres.	Ascoglossum x Phalaenopsis x Renanthera
Hawkinsara	Hknsa.	Broughtonia x Cattleya x Laelia x Sophronitis
Maclellanara	Mclna.	Brassia x Odontoglossum x Oncidium
Mizutaara	Miz.	Cattleya x Diacrium x Schomburgkia
Otaara	Otr.	Broughtonia x Brassavola x Cattleya x Laelia
Potinara	Pot.	Brassavola x Cattleya x Laelia x Sophronitis
Recchara	Recc.	Brassavola x Cattleya x Laelia x Schomburgkia
Schombocatonia	Smbcna.	Broughtonia x Cattleya x Schomburgkia
Sophrolaeliocattleya	Slc.	Cattleya x Laelia x Sophronitis
Wilburchangara	Wbchg.	Broughtonia x Cattleya x Epidendrum x Schomburgkia

Intergeneric hybrids add spice to the variety of orchids from which hobbyists may choose. This is especially true of the *Cattleya* Alliance, a group of related genera originally from the New World Tropics — *Cattleya, Laelia, Sophronitis* and others — that may be hybridized with one another with a tremendous amount of success. Consider the example shown above: *Sophrolaeliocattleya* Jinn (top left) was crossed with *Laeliocattleya* Trick or Treat (top right) to yield the intergeneric hybrid *Sophrolaeliocattleya* Sixpence. One cultivar of *Slc.* Sixpence (above) was given the cultivar name 'TNT', to distinguish it from other cultivars. When propagated vegetatively — through division or micropropagation techniques — all plants of *Slc.* Sixpence 'TNT', FCC/AOS, will bear the same name and be genetically identical. Growers: *Slc.* Jinn 'Yellow Sparkler', JC/AOS — the late James Nickou, DDS; *Lc.* Trick or Treat 'Lea', HCC/AOS — Richard Takafuji; *Slc.* Sixpence 'TNT', FCC/AOS — Bill Stephens and Grover Heisley.

Orchid Names

By James B. Watson

UNDERSTANDING ORCHID NAMES enhances the pleasure of this hobby. Initially, it is easy to talk with friends using common names like moth orchids and lady's-slipper orchids. But eventually, one needs to come to grips with botanical names. Though they are perhaps intimidating at first, mastering the simple Latin of scientific names will eliminate the twist from the tongue and enable everyone to talk about orchids with confidence.

Parts of a Name To elucidate an orchid's name, pick up a catalog or plant label from one of your plants. Most likely, the name will consist of at least two words. The first is the name of the genus (plural: genera). It is usually printed in italics because, as Latin, it is a foreign language, and begins with a capital letter (*Cattleya, Epidendrum, Zygopetalum*). Botanists abbreviate generic names with the first letter (such as *C.* for *Cattleya* and *E.* for *Epidendrum*), while horticulturists often use short abbreviations, such as *Epi.* for *Epidendrum* and *Phal.* for *Phalaenopsis*.

Within each genus there may be dozens, if not hundreds, of variations on a theme. Taxonomists recognize these species by giving them individual names called specific epithets (these usually begin with a lower-case letter and are also in italics). A specific epithet may indicate place of origin (*costaricensis*, from Costa Rica), the person who found the orchid (*besseae*, for Libby Besse), a characteristic of the orchid (*glabra*, for smooth) or might honor an individual (*garayi*, for Leslie Garay). Together, the genus name and specific epithet compose the species name, and often impart a bit of information. Hence, *Masdevallia coccinea* is a species with red flowers (*coccinea* means red) and *Paphiopedilum philippinense* was discovered in the Philippines.

Some species may exhibit certain characteristics with additional variation that a taxonomist can recognize by assigning a subspecies, varietal or form name. These begin with a lower-case letter, are in italics and are the third name in the sequence. The flowers of *Phragmipedium besseae* are typically red, but a variant with yellow flowers has been named *Phragmipedium besseae* var. *flavum*.

A major attraction of orchids is the diversity of hybrids available to growers. Hybrids have names, too. When a hybrid is made, the breeder, or his or her representative, assigns a grex or group name that applies to all of the hybrid progeny. A grex name begins with a capital letter and is in Roman type. When *Paphiopedilum niveum* was crossed with *Paphiopedilum tonsum*, all progeny were given the name *Paphiopedilum* Olivia.

Because this cross was registered in 1898, some plants with exceptionally fine flowers have been observed and assigned cultivar names to distinguish them. When researching *Paph.* Olivia in the literature, one might see the cultivar names 'Lorelei', HCC/AOS, or 'Casa Luna', AM/AOS, following the grex name.

Cultivar names may be applied to hybrids (*Paph.* Olivia 'Lorelei', HCC/AOS) as well as species (*Paphiopedilum appletonianum* 'Seascape', HCC/AOS). A cultivar name begins with a capital letter, is in Roman type and set within single quotation marks. When vegetatively propagated — through divisions, keikis (offshoots) or mericlones — all derivatives of a cultivar will be genetically identical and possess the same cultivar name. This permits hobbyists to know exactly what to expect from a plant they purchase bearing this name.

Glancing at the clonal names above reveals some extra letters — such as AM/AOS and HCC/AOS — following the plants' names. These indicate an award, in this case granted by the American Orchid Soci-

The Old World genus *Paphiopedilum* contains approximately 60 species and countless hybrids. When two species — *Paph. niveum* (top left) and *Paph. tonsum* (top right) — were crossed, the hybrid was given the grex name *Paphiopedium* Olivia. To distinguish selected forms of the progeny, some clones were given cultivar names, such as *Paph.* Olivia 'Solo's Springtime',

HCC/AOS (above), grown by Sophie and Lou Martin. The HCC following the cultivar name indicates a flower quality award granted by the American Orchid Society (AOS). Each of the species above also have cultivar names. Growers: *Paph. niveum* 'Catatonk', HCC/AOS — Lynn and Bob Wellenstein; *Paph. tonsum* 'Lambert Day', HCC/AOS — S.R. Weltz Jr.

ety (AOS). These awards, which are discussed on page 16, may be given to both species and hybrids. The letters before the slash are an abbreviation for the award; AM is an Award of Merit, HCC a Highly Commended Certificate. The letters following the slash indicate the association that bestowed the award. Awards are given by several organizations, including the American Orchid Society (AOS), The Royal Horticultural Society (RHS), the South Florida Orchid Society (SFOS) and the Hawaiian Orchid Society (HOS). An award imparts prestige, and, generally, a higher price.

A thorough discussion of orchid nomenclature is presented in *The Handbook on Orchid Nomenclature and Registration* (4th edition, 1993), prepared by The Handbook Committee of the International Orchid Commission with the cooperation of The Royal Horticultural Society.

Pronunciation Arguing the correct pronunciation of potato and tomato is nothing compared with some of the heated debates surrounding the proper way to pronounce botanical Latin. Fortunately, many basic orchid names are agreed upon. With a modicum of effort, they become a part of the enthusiastic orchidist's vocabulary. The key to success: talk with fellow orchidists at meetings, shows, nurseries and regional judging sessions. Listen to others. Take the time to practice yourself. And invest in one of several guides that offer invaluable advice for pronouncing names, and, frequently, their meaning, too. Some of these are the American Orchid Society's *Illustrated Orchid Dictionary* (2002 Edition) and Alex Hawkes' *Encyclopaedia of Cultivated Orchids* (1965).

(James B. Watson is director of publications at the American Orchid Society.)

Common Names

HOBBYISTS OFTEN coin common names for orchids to facilitate communication among their peers. Below are some of the more frequently encountered common names with their botanical equivalents.

Common Name	Botanical Name
Bamboo orchid	*Arundina graminifolia*
Bee orchid	*Luisia, Ophrys apifera*
Braided orchid	*Lockhartia* species
Bucket orchid	*Coryanthes* species
Butterfly orchid	*Oncidium papilio*
Christmas star orchid	*Angraecum sesquipedale*
Cigar orchid	*Cyrtopodium punctatum*
Cow-horn orchid	*Cyrtopodium punctatum, Schomburgkia tibicinis*
Dancing-lady orchid	*Oncidium* species
Dove orchid (Dove flower)	*Peristeria elata*
Frog orchid	*Polyrrhiza lindenii, Coeloglossum viride, Habenaria viridis*
Ghost orchid	*Polyrrhiza lindenii*
Grass pink	*Calopogon tuberosus*
Jewel orchids	*Anoectochilus, Dossinia, Goodyera, Ludisia* species
Ladies' tresses	*Spiranthes* species
Lady-of-the-night orchid	*Brassavola nodosa, Epidendrum nocturnum*
Lady's-slipper	*Cypripedium, Paphiopedilum, Phragmipedium, Selenipedium*
Moth orchid	*Phalaenopsis*
Mule-ear orchid	*Oncidium luridum*
Nun's orchid (Nun's lily)	*Phaius tankervilleae* (syn. *Phaius grandifolius*)
Pansy orchid	*Miltoniopsis* species
Spider orchids	*Arachnis, Brassia, Epidendrum ciliare, Caladenia*
Star-of-Bethlehem orchid	*Angraecum sesquipedale*
Swan orchid	*Cycnoches*, especially *Cycnoches chlorochilon*
Tulip orchid	*Anguloa*, especially *Anguloa clowesii*

— Compiled by S. H. Yearron

The Benefits of Judging Orchids

BRINGING AN ORCHID TO BLOOM is an achievement of which every beginning grower can be proud. And, at first, each plant seems worth its weight in diamonds. After several years' experience in the orchid world, the beginner comes to realize that there are some orchids more intriguing, more treasured and more beautiful than others. These "better" orchids — compared to those of previous years — represent the attainment of certain standards of form and color and, as such, are singled out for certain honors.

These standards are determined and applied by the American Orchid Society. The organization has developed a system for judging better orchids which seeks to grant recognition to superior forms of orchid species and hybrids; recognize the development of improved hybrid forms; encourage meritorious trends in hybridizing; and reward horticultural skill in orchid

Growers Dick and Carol Doran's horticultural skills were recognized when their *Sophronitis coccinea* 'Cora', CCM/AOS, received a Certificate of Cultural Merit (top). The HCC following *Paphiopedilum* Francisco Freire 'Jamboree Gold', HCC/AOS (*sukhakulii* x *godefroyae*) (above), indicates this hybrid received a Highly Commended Certificate, a quality award granted to flowers scoring between 75 and 79 points. Grower: Paphanatics, unLtd.

growing. Highly trained and experienced American Orchid Society judges conduct monthly judging sessions throughout the United States to which orchid growers may bring any orchid. The judges carefully evaluate each plant and flower from many different aspects, offering a final collective opinion. If an entry fulfills any of the above requirements to an outstanding degree, the judges may award it one or more of 10 awards.

In this guide, initials are placed after many orchids' names; for example, *Paphiopedilum appletonianum* 'Seascape', HCC/AOS. The awards and their significance are:

AD (Award of Distinction) and AQ (Award of Quality) • These awards for breeding recognize worthy new trends and improved quality, respectively.

AM (Award of Merit) • A flower scoring 80 to 89 points on a 100-point scale. This flower-quality award is a fine, though lesser, achievement than the FCC.

CBR (Certificate of Botanical Recognition) • Awarded to rare and unusual species with educational interest.

CCE (Certificate of Cultural Excellence) • This award further distinguishes growers of plants that exhibit an extreme degree of skill in cultivation, having received 90 points or more on the scale that has been used for the Certificate of Cultural Merit (CCM).

CCM (Certificate of Cultural Merit) • The beginning orchid grower can hope to attain this award because, this award, rather than designating an individual flower of high quality, recognizes the grower and not the plant. The CCM/AOS may be given more than once if the plant continues to thrive and increase in both the size and number of flowers.

CHM (Certificate of Horticultural Merit) • Awarded to a well-grown and well-flowered species or natural hybrid with characteristics that contribute to the horticultural aspects of orchidology, such as aesthetic appeal.

FCC (First Class Certificate) • The highest flower-quality award, given to flowers scoring 90 points or more on a 100-point scale.

HCC (Highly Commended Certificate) • The HCC is granted to a flower scoring 75 to 79 points on a 100-point scale, which is not enough points to garner an AM. The great majority of awarded orchids receive this award, which implies that, while the flower is outstanding, there is room for improvement.

JC (Judges' Commendation) • This award is given for distinctive characteristics that the judges unanimously feel should be recognized but cannot be scored in the customary ways.

Where Orchids are Judged

THE AMERICAN Orchid Society maintains an elaborate network of approximately 560 certified judges, who grant numerous types of awards to deserving orchid species and hybrids and to exhibits under rules defined in the Society's *Handbook on Judging and Exhibition*. This invaluable reference tool describes the regulations necessary to receive awards and the process of becoming an orchid judge, and explains how to organize an orchid show.

Most orchid shows are staged at definite times of the year and hence many outstanding plants cannot be displayed and judged because their blooming periods do not coincide with a show. To remedy this situation, the American Orchid Society has established a number of Regional Judging Centers where orchids may be brought or sent for judging. The centers and their meeting times and dates are listed in each monthly issue of *Orchids*.

Orchid growers within traveling distance often bring their plants or flowers to be judged, but orchid growers anywhere in the world may send their flowers by air. These sessions also often include a discussion on orchid evaluation or a similarly educational program, thereby improving the knowledge of attending judges.

Complete details on the American Orchid Society judging system and how to become a judge are available from the Society's International Orchid Center.

CULTURE

© CHARLES MARDEN FITCH

Phragmipedium Grande (*caudatum* x *longifolium*)
lives up to its name when its glorious flowers
unfurl. Diffused light, adequate moisture and
warm temperatures induce this terrestrial to
bloom. *Phragmipedium* Grande 'Giganteum',
CCM/AOS, is one of several awarded forms of
this primary hybrid.
Grower: Marilyn Mirro.

Orchids in the Home

By judywhite

MANY ORCHIDS ARE REWARDING indoor plants. Once a homeowner has succumbed and bought his or her first orchid, or received one as a gift, meeting a few cultural requirements will coax the plant to flower again.

Orchids are far tougher and hardier than most people think, and are, by and large, extremely adaptable. There is a long-standing myth that orchids are difficult, if not impossible, to grow, especially without a greenhouse. With at least 25,000 species and some 110,000 artifical hybrids, there are some notoriously fussy orchids. But there are many rugged, popular, easy-to-grow types that adapt to the temperatures and light conditions found on the average home windowsill. Explore the options and assemble a collection that will put forth exotic flowers year round.

Orchids are different from other houseplants. Unlike ferns, philodendrons, palms and Swedish ivy, orchids do not grow in soil. Potting an orchid in soil is actually one of the best ways to kill it. Most orchids in the wild are not rooted in the ground, but instead attach themselves by thick roots to tree trunks and branches. Clinging to the bark, the plants absorb water and nutrients from the air and rain and whatever drips down the tree. They are adapted to surviving when the rain is scarce, hoarding water in thick leaves, stems and roots.

Watering   In the house, orchids are grown in pots filled with chips of bark, stones, tree fern or some other loosely packed material, which keeps roots well-aerated and permits water to drain quickly. Nothing — repeat, nothing — kills an orchid faster than letting it sit in a water-logged pot, because a lack of oxygen will cause the roots to suffocate and rot.

Water orchids thoroughly, usually about once a week, then allow them to dry slightly before watering again. Orchids are better equipped to withstand periods of forgetfulness than they are to being overwatered.

Temperature   Another difference between orchids and many houseplants is that in nature most orchids experience a big difference between day and night temperatures. Manipulating the temperature of the home so it will drop at least 10 degrees at night, especially in autumn and winter when many orchids initiate buds, will induce the orchids to set flower buds more readily. Achieve this by lowering the temperature

© CHARLES MARDEN FITCH

With the arrival of spring, many orchids burst into bloom. One of the most popular orchids for indoor growing is the phalaenopsis, or moth orchid, which is cherished for its sprays of colorful flowers that remain fresh for months (opposite center). Equally dazzling are the lower-growing *nobile*-type dendrobiums, whose abundant delicate flowers clothe the upright pseudobulbs.

Orchids thrive in a humid atmosphere. In the home, mist the plants or set them on trays filled with gravel and water. Adjust the water level so it comes to just below the surface of the gravel.

on the thermostat. This little trick can mean the difference between an orchid plant that lives, and one that thrives and flowers.

Orchids are usually classified as warm growing, intermediate and cool growing, with regard to their temperature needs. Many tolerate exposure to warmer or cooler temperatures without suffering damage. The temperature groupings refer to the lowest temperature the orchid prefers during winter nights. Warm-growing orchids, such as phalaenopsis, sulk if temperatures drop much below 60 F. Intermediate growers, such as cattleyas, prefer winter nights around 55 F. Cool-growing orchids, including cymbidiums and odontoglossums, are accustomed to winter nights of 50 F. At the other extreme, most orchids perform poorly when exposed to temperatures above 90 F.

Light Orchids are also classified into three other groups depending on the intensity of light they require — high (3,000 foot-candles), medium (2,000 foot-candles) and low (1,000 to 1,500 foot-candles). Most orchids require plenty of light, preferably at least six hours a day. Many orchids can withstand more or less than the amount of recommended light, but providing more light enhances flowering potential. Conversely, inadequate light prevents orchids from flowering, although they will grow.

Leaf color indicates if the amount of light is adequate. The lush, rich, dark green of most houseplants is not desirable in orchid leaves. Dark green leaves are attractive, but signal there is not enough light. A grassy green color (light or medium green with yellowish tones) means the plant is receiving sufficient light to bloom. Gauge light intensity with this simple hand/eye test: Put your hand 6 inches above the leaves and look at the shadows cast. A sharp-edged shadow means high light; a soft-edged shadow indicates medium to low light; no shadow at all means the light is insufficient for an orchid to flower.

Southern- and eastern-facing windows work best for orchids; western windows can be too hot in the afternoon; and northern ones are usually too dark. Too much direct light causes leaves to sunburn — the leaves bleach out to white, ultimately dying and turning black — so it may be necessary to reposition plants as the seasons change. Move plants away from or toward the window to manipulate the amount of light. A sheer curtain will cast light shade. Positioning sheets of Mylar or another reflective material in the growing area will increase usable light, a handy trick for the winter when light levels are often reduced.

Artificial Light Where windows with adequate light are unavailable, consider cultivating orchids beneath artificial light. Four 4-foot-long fluorescent tubes placed 6 inches apart side by side should do the trick. Two shop-light fixtures with cool-white bulbs will suffice. Special grow lights, sold under various trade names, are consider-

© CHARLES MARDEN FITCH

To measure temperatures accurately, invest in maximum-minimum thermometers, which are recommended for evaluating the environments of microclimates.

ably more expensive, and extend the light spectrum. The grow lights may reap better results, although data on this are conflicting. Place plants 6 to 8 inches below the tubes. Put the lights on a timer set to operate the bulbs for 14 to 16 hours a day. Many orchids, such as phalaenopsis and paphiopedilums, will be content. Orchids requiring more light, such as vandas and cymbidiums, however, need natural sunlight or high-intensity discharge lights to bloom.

A fluorescent fixture in a dimly lit window adds extra light to natural sunlight, too, and can mean the difference between flowers and no flowers. Orchids that do not flower often require more light.

Fertilizing Orchids do not require abundant doses of fertilizer. However, to maintain healthy plants and see blooms on a regular basis, apply a weak solution of 20-20-20 fertilizer once a week. Each month, water with plain water to flush out any accumulated fertilizer salts. Dilute the fertilizer to one-quarter the strength recommended on the package. When in doubt, give less rather than more.

With a little imagination, a basement or unused room can become home to orchids — even if there is no natural light. Orchid enthusiasts often develop growing areas to meet the needs of their expanding collections. Here, an apartment dweller installed shelves illuminated with broad-spectrum fluorescent tubes. A timer turns the lights on and off automatically.

Switch to a blossom-booster fertilizer in the autumn, when many orchids are initiating flower buds. Blossom-booster is a fertilizer ratio with higher phosphorus and lower nitrogen, such as a 10-30-20 formula. Many orchids are winter bloomers, which makes them even more special as houseplants. They fill an often otherwise flowerless void in the drabbest of months. Peak of orchid bloom usually occurs between December and April.

Humidity One of the things orchids greatly appreciate is adequate humidity. Fifty percent or more is necessary, but the atmosphere in most homes, especially those with dry, hot-air heat, is far below that. Raising the humidity around orchids will result in better flowering. Some tricks to increase humidity: operate a humidifier near the plants; place the pots on flat, black pebbles set in a tray in which water is added until it almost covers the stones ("Egg crate," which is the lattice-like plastic grid sold in hardware stores for suspension ceiling lights, is a good, more steady alternative to the pebbles.); group the orchids together; or cordon off the growing area with clear plastic (but continue to provide ventilation to prevent bacteria from becoming a problem).

High humidity, however, can create a host of problems, such as fungal diseases and bacterial infections that mar foliage and flowers alike. Natural, healthy orchid environments are full of breezes which counteract these potential hazards. Sufficient air movement is essential to keep them at bay in the home. Small fans keep the air buoyant; switching their location and direction every once in a while emulates natural breezes. If the orchid-growing

Building a Collection

■ Read *Orchids — The Magazine of the American Orchid Society*, which is filled with ads from orchid nurseries. Some firms issue catalogs with photographs and many descriptions; smaller firms often offer only a list with names and prices. Any charge for a catalog is usually refunded with the first order. Some nurseries maintain sites on the World Wide Web.

■ Visit local greenhouses and nurseries. There is no better way to get an idea of plant and flower size. Visiting in person enables one to see many flowers simultaneously. Commercial growers provide helpful answers when asked to suggest plants that will do well in particular environments.

■ Consult the listing of commercial growers in the *American Orchid Society Orchid Source Directory*. It lists various orchid firms, large and small, by state and country. Keep a copy of this handy resource in the car. Any trip can be made to fit around a conveniently located nursery. The directory is sent to all AOS members and also given to new members. Copies are available through The AOS BookShop.

■ Attend orchid shows and other plant sales. Orchid shows are full of plants in flower and booths managed by vendors ready to dispense cultural information, plants, books and accoutrements.

■ Join a local orchid society. The meetings are good sources of new plants, whether by door prizes, raffles, annual auctions and shows; communal plant orders that yield big discounts; or the visiting guest speakers who are also commercial vendors and bring a load of plants to sell.

© CHARLES MARDEN FITCH

Mail-order nurseries can ship orchids of any size worldwide. Careful packing techniques guarantee safe arrival.

■ Talk to fellow orchid growers. Club members often divide plants to give away or sell among themselves. When a desirable orchid is seen on the show table at a monthly meeting, ask the owner if he or she plans to divide it soon, and make deals. Once a plant collection is assembled, arrange trades for future acquisitions.

environment feels and smells healthy and fresh, chances are it is meeting the orchids' needs.

Popular Selections Some of the easiest orchids to grow are also among the showiest and most popular. Beginners are advised to buy blooming-size plants, because small seedlings sometimes take five years before finally sending up a flower.

When the public thinks of an orchid, it is most likely the *Cattleya*. Cattleyas are flashy and magnificent, and often extremely fragrant, a surprise to people only familiar with them as cut flowers. The fragrance fades after the flower is picked. In fact, a *Cattleya* species is the source of the fragrance in Joy, one of the most expensive perfumes. Standard cattleyas are 2- to 3-foot-tall ungainly plants, but recent hybridizing efforts have yielded 8- to 12-inch-tall wonders, still packed with good-sized flowers. These are known as compact cattleyas or mini-catts, and are worth asking for. *Cattleya* hybrids often bloom twice a year, bearing flowers that last about three weeks.

Cattleyas are good choices for bright-to-medium light conditions. They are the camels of the orchid world, able to withstand drought. Cattleya relatives, interrelated and interbred, include *Cattleya* (abbreviated in catalogs and labels as *C.*), *Laelia* (*L.*), *Brassolaeliocattleya* (*Blc.*) and *Sophrolaeliocattleya* (*Slc.*), among others. In catalogs, fortunately, they are usually all lumped together under the main category of *Cattleya* Alliance, and growers know what hobbyists mean when a cattleya type is requested. Cattleyas are tough to beat when in flower, but not gorgeous when out of bloom. Anyone interested in prettier foliage is guided to phalaenopsis, mottled-leaved paphiopedilums and miltoniopsis.

One of the most elegant of all orchids is the formidable sounding *Phalaenopsis*, or phal, for short. Phalaenopsis send up long arching inflorescences of lovely flowers that last an incredible three months or more. Typical colors are the larger-flowered whites and pinks, often spotted or

When watering orchids in a sink, place the container on a plastic mesh tray to keep the potting mix from washing into the drain. A sprinkler attached to a flexible hose makes it easy to direct water onto the medium.

© CHARLES MARDEN FITCH

striped, but there are now also smaller yellows, greens and reds. A few phalaenopsis, including *Phalaenopsis schilleriana* and *Phalaenopsis violacea*, are fragrant.

Phalaenopsis require less light than cattleyas, which places them in the low-light category. Water them more frequently than cattleyas, and never allow the medium to dry completely. They cannot be divided, unless by chance they produce an offset (keiki), similar to a stolon produced by a spider plant.

Beautiful mottled foliage is characteristic of some species and hybrids of *Paphiopedilum*, or lady's-slipper orchids. Paphiopedilums bear odd flowers with pouches that make them appear exotic. Their unusual good looks are expressed in reds, greens, whites, yellows and beiges, often with stripes and weird spotted "warts." The flowers last for months.

Paphiopedilums, called paphs for short, require low to medium levels of light, and usually can grow side by side with phalaenopsis. They are a bit different than many orchids because most do not grow on trees, but rather in the ground — not in dirt, but

Phalaenopsis are the perfect choice for the homeowner wishing to raise orchids on the windowsill. There are dozens of hybrids from which to choose, ranging in size and flower color, such as Phalaenopsis Memoria Marian Cohen 'Goodie', HCC/AOS (Golden Penang x Golden Duplicate). Grower: San Diego Orchid.

in loose leaf mold. Pot them in containers filled with bark chips that are a bit smaller than those recommended for other orchids, and keep them moist.

In cooler climes, watch for *Miltoniopsis,* or pansy orchid, with arching grass-like foliage. Miltoniopsis flowers mimic pansies, often with garish-colored patterns on their lips. Medium light and a constantly moist medium suit them. The other orchids mentioned previously make long-lasting cut flowers, but miltoniopsis do not. Miltoniopsis, like paphiopedilums and phalaenopsis, grow reliably beneath lights.

Commercial growers are meeting the needs of homeowners for more orchids. Trips to garden centers, even the grocery store, now warrant a visit to the plant area where orchids are often found. Evergreen dendrobiums are typical sights in the autumn, when their graceful sprays of purple,

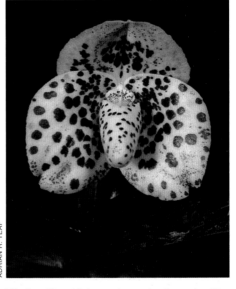

HUGH B. HENRY

ADRIAN R. TEAF

Newcomers to the world of orchids may want to begin with cattleyas, including *Cattleya* Marie Riopelle 'Ocean View', AM/AOS (Empress Bells x Douglas Johnston). Although the best light conditions for cattleyas are often in greenhouses, positioning cattleyas in south-facing windows inside the home can induce plants to flower.

lavender, pink and white flowers arch from the reed-like stems. At other times of year, oncidiums, or dancing-lady orchids, garner attention with their delicate flowers in shades of yellow, orange, red, pink and white. And there are cymbidiums, hefty grass-like plants with sprays of waxy flowers rendered in hues of green, yellow and soft pastels. A visit to an orchid nursery or annual show and sale of a local orchid society is a terrific way to view and purchase a great diversity of orchids.

Hardy and rewarding, orchids are priced to fit the budget and guaranteed to bring a wealth of admiration. No wonder orchids are the reigning royalty of the flower world. Just about anyone can grow Swedish ivy. But, ahh, to grow an orchid.

(*judywhite is author of* Tayor's Guide to Orchids, *which was published in 1996.*)

Windowsill and light-garden enthusiasts should investigate paphiopedilums, such as *Paphiopedilum bellatulum.* The cultivar 'Babs', AM/AOS, was grown by Michael Bowell. Unlike many orchids, paphiopedilums possess attractive foliage — which may be green or mottled — so they look great even when not in bloom. Warm temperatures and a constant supply of moisture induce these durable orchids to flower and provide splashes of color year-round.

Orchids Under Artificial Light

By Howard W. Zoufaly

ARTIFICIAL LIGHTS CREATE THE perfect environment in which to grow orchids for the hobbyist with limited space. The lights can be a simple substitute for unavailable natural light or a complex fusion of various light sources scientifically created to mimic nature's way.

Most orchid growers who turn to artificial light do so after exhausting suitable window ledges for their ever-expanding hobby or because an under-utilized corner of a room or basement seems an ideal place to begin this fascinating hobby. For whatever reason one decides to grow orchids under artificial lights, a vast number of species and hybrids of numerous genera can be successfully raised and flowered without natural light if the grower recognizes the needs of the plants and follows normal good cultural habits. The rules of orchid culture do not change for light gardening but need only be altered to fit the unique circumstances. With this in mind, it is possible to cultivate ascocendas, cattleyas, miltonias, odontoglossums, oncidiums, paphiopedilums, phalaenopsis and other low-light and medium-light orchids.

Naturally, the most important considerations are the type of lights and the fixtures in which they are housed.

Lighting and Equipment For the beginner and most hobbyists, there is a wide choice of specially designed fluorescent tubes. All offer a balance of the red and blue side of the light spectrum necessary for growth and flowering. Tubes should be of the 40-watt variety; group a minimum of four together for healthy growth. It is almost impossible to gain too much light from fluorescents, but quite normal to overestimate the amount provided. Among the most popular tubes are Glo-Lux Wide Spectrum, Naturescent, Vita-Lite and Vita-Lite Powertwist. The latter have greater output due to their unique construction. Verilux Tru-Bloom bulbs, originally designed for use in museums, are also ideal because they copy the sun's spectrum and mimic the appearance of natural light.

Select fixtures that are economical. There are a number of commercial light carts available for home use which are ideal for the new grower because they offer racks, trays and fixtures in one package. For those with a do-it-yourself mentality, shop lights (available in hardware stores) can be combined with a limited amount of lumber to serve an equal purpose.

Other types of lights can be adapted to orchid culture. GTE Sylvania produces Maxi-Grow B bulbs for special fixtures which are now used by commercial as well as amateur growers quite successfully. These sodium-vapor-type bulbs are well-suited for anyone planning to grow different types of orchids, especially those whose growth habits make them unsuitable for fluorescents. Sodium-vapor lights are also available in pre-built plant stands that make installation and maintenance easier. ITT Outdoor Lighting Division manufactures a quartz yard-light with a 300-watt bulb that looks somewhat like a pencil and which this author has used successfully for several years. It can be angled to illuminate several dozen plants in an area which would require six to eight fluorescent tubes.

Some of the above lights do require installation by an electrician. In addition, they may produce considerable heat which may burn plants, and, for this reason, care must be taken with their use. They are best suited for growers with some experience.

Temperature Orchids need a minimum 10-degree change between day and night temperatures. Most homes easily can provide this. To accommodate a mixed collection of cool-growing and warm-growing orchids, place those with lower temperature needs closer to the floor.

Any homeowner faced with a space-crunch can find rewarding flowering plants in the orchid family. One solution: compact masdevallias topped with charming flowers in a rainbow of colors, including *Masdevallia minuta* 'Fox Den', CBR/AOS. Grower: H. Phillips Jesup.

© CHARLES MARDEN FITCH

Humidity Modern homes are dry, especially those in the north with hot-air heat. Place the orchids on a tray filled with gravel and filled with water up to the surface of the rocks. But take care the pots are not in the water. In a basement room, line the room with plastic, which will help hold moisture. Many commercial plant stands can be purchased with a plastic tent for this purpose.

Ventilation Even in the humid jungle, there are gentle winds which keep plants healthy. A fan will help move air, reduce bacterial disease problems and result in better growth. Unfortunately, air-conditioned homes are not ideal. Try to keep plants away from the blowers in homes so equipped. An open window is beneficial when the weather outdoors is warm.

Watering Orchids under lights in the home dry out at different rates than the same plants in nature. In winter, hot dry air in the home may necessitate more frequent watering. Follow the cultural needs of the type of plants being grown. The easiest way to control water is to use trays with a single drainage hole at one end. Water that drips out can be caught in a bucket and easily thrown out. Some trays come with a plastic stopper, the bottom of which can be cut off with a knife and fitted with plastic tubes to direct water downward without splashing. This is especially handy if plants are growing on several levels.

Special Considerations It is hard to determine how much light plants are receiving because normal light meters do not give an accurate reading with plant-type bulbs. It is safe to estimate that a single fluorescent tube will produce 1,000 foot-candles of light 2 inches from the center. This amount will be increased with greater numbers of tubes. Low-light orchids require a minimum of 1,500 foot-candles per day, which means a two-bulb setup should be operated each day. A timer is extremely important. The hours of light can be adjusted to follow natural sunlight, increasing the hours beyond that of the sun for better growth. Twenty hours of light in summer, decreased to 10 in winter, works ideally for this author.

High-Intensity-Discharge Lamps More and more growers are using HID lighting for orchids. These bulbs cast stronger light than fluorescent bulbs, making it necessary to place plants farther away from the light source. Special track systems are available that move fixtures to cast uniform light and help prevent plants from overheating. Special wiring and the skills of an electrician may be necessary for some setups. However, newer units can be plugged into regular electrical outlets. Cultivating orchids under HID lighting requires growing practices different from those prescribed for fluorescent-bulb culture.

(Howard W. Zoufaly has written about growing orchids under lights for various publications of the American Orchid Society.)

Orchids in the Greenhouse

ELVIN MCDONALD

GREENHOUSES RUN THE GAMUT from elegant conservatories to compact window greenhouses that fit snugly into a kitchen window frame. Whatever the size, similar suggestions for selection, design and installation apply.

There are three major types of greenhouses to consider.

• The lean-to greenhouse is usually small, about 6 to 10 feet wide, and 10 to 12 feet long. One of its long sides is formed by the side of the house to which it is attached. Relatively inexpensive to make and maintain, its major drawbacks are a lack of space for an expanding collection and a tendency to heat up and cool off more rapidly than is desirable.

• The attached greenhouse is an extension of one's home, connected at the narrow end rather than the long side, as with the lean-to greenhouse. It is generally large and thus capable of providing more reasonable control over humidity, ventilation and

Phalaenopsis fill the greenhouse with a spectacular riot of color each spring. Grower: Zuma Canyon Orchids, Inc.

expansion problems. Some homeowners incorporate a living area into a lean-to or attached greenhouse.

• The free-standing greenhouse is unattached on all four sides. It is the most expensive to construct but, aside from some inconvenience of access in inclement weather, it offers maximum light and the best control. Some space must be sacrificed for a work bench and storage area.

Visit as many orchid greenhouses as possible, and consult books on and manufacturers of greenhouses before making a final decision.

Where space is limited inside the home, window greenhouses offer a prime space in which to cultivate small-growing orchids. Opt for a model with vents and small fans that enhance ventilation. Two or three shelves increase space; they may be solid, to prevent water from dripping on the plants below, or perforated to aid air circulation.

Size The optimum size with which to begin is a greenhouse 14 feet wide and 14 to 20 feet long. This affords a center bench as well as two side benches. Such a greenhouse may seem enormous at first, and unnecessary for an initial collection, but there are several factors to consider. First, those contemplating a greenhouse are serious about orchid growing. Consequently, the collection will inevitably grow by leaps and bounds. What seems to be adequate space today will become a major limitation in two years. Second, since a large greenhouse is preferable in the long run, it is less expensive to build it now than to add an extension onto a smaller one in the future.

Light Regardless of the type, locate the greenhouse to capture maximum light. The best position for a free-standing one is on a north-south axis so that the sun travels across the entire length as it moves from east to west. A lean-to or attached greenhouse should also have a maximum exposure, east or south, but never north. Avoid nearby shade trees or shadows from adjacent homes or buildings. It is easy to cut down on light that is too intense; it is relatively impossible, however, to provide light when the greenhouse is shaded by forces beyond the owner's control. In planning the construction of a greenhouse there are a number of factors to be considered. Most demand professional advice.

Structure The foundation of a greenhouse is an additional but necessary expense. All greenhouses should have one. In areas where temperatures dip below 35 F, the foundation, whether of poured concrete, brick or cinder, must extend well below the frost line. Otherwise, the greenhouse will warp and twist. The floor is always the leveled earth, never a slab of concrete, thus ensuring proper drainage. A clay-earth floor may be covered with several inches of cinders or gravel.

Benches Construct the height and width of benches for convenience, gener-

ally 30 inches tall and 33 inches wide. The center bench may be twice this width as it is accessible from two sides. Select treated lumber that is resistant to moisture, or aluminum and steel, which have proven more durable, even though initially they are more expensive. The top surface of the benches should provide aeration and so should be formed either by redwood or cypress strips, spaced about their own width apart, or by a strong aluminum mesh. Air can thus circulate upward through the pots.

Heating A heating system is essential in any area that has recorded temperatures below 45 F. It is wise to provide an emergency heater as well. Too many collections have been lost to freezing due to oversights, power failures or lack of proper maintenance of the heating system. A wide choice of heating systems is available: steam, circulating hot water, ducted hot air, natural gas. Where bottled gas must be used, absolutely no fumes should penetrate into the greenhouse. Orchids are notoriously susceptible to ethylene gas and will soon die if any is present.

Cooling and Ventilation Except in very warm climates, a cooling system is usually not essential, because manual ventilation is adequate for those extra warm days. To grow odontoglossums and similar cool-growing genera, it may be advantageous, even necessary, to invest in an evaporative cooler in order to provide the low temperatures these orchids require. Automatic humidifying devices are necessary and should run in conjunction with adequate ventilation mechanisms. Side and roof vents operated automatically or manually, in addition to several fans running continuously, will keep the moisture-laden air moving freely throughout the greenhouse. Shading will depend largely on the characteristics of the particular climate and will have to be adjusted accordingly.

Several good reference books are available that explain how to design and build greenhouses and cultivate a variety of orchids successfully.

Repotting Orchids

By Stephen R. Batchelor

REPOTTING IS A NECESSARY ELE-ment of a wise health-care program. The organic media, in which orchids are rooted, decompose into humus, a material, by it-self, unfit for orchid roots. In a decomposed medium, roots rarely have adequate oxy-gen to survive and function. Repot before significant media decomposition occurs to avoid major root loss.

Cattleyas, laelias, encyclias and other fast-growing sympodial orchids (those which grow horizontally by rhizomes) may need repotting before media decomposi-tion. One of these that has grown beyond the edge of its container will require repotting and/or dividing before the rhi-zomes and roots become a tangled mass.

Knowing When to Repot Decide whether an orchid could produce new roots at the time of repotting. Most complex *Cattleya* hybrids are capable of forming new roots nearly any time. Even so, repotting a plant with an actively expand-ing pseudobulb just beginning or about to produce its own cluster of roots is ideal.

Emerging new roots with bright green tips signal that it is time to repot, but do so before the roots are 1 inch long to prevent breaking them.

© CHARLES MARDEN FITCH

Such practice often means quick establish-ment in the new medium. To wait until root development on the new growth is nearly completed is less than ideal, because an-other such flush of new, penetrating root growth is unlikely and those newer roots will be exposed, like the rest, to mechanical damage in repotting.

Proper timing of repotting also consid-ers the flowering period of the orchid in-volved. Because a change of medium is to some degree a shock to a plant, repotting at a time when an orchid is in bud or flower is risky. Bud drop may result if repotting is done during the period of bud develop-ment. At the very least, some lessening in the ultimate size and longevity of the flow-ers is apt to occur. Repot most orchids when new growths and roots emerge, which is typically after flowering.

Timing repotting to coincide with a period of active root development is not always possible, due to a dangerously de-composed medium. In this case, it is far better to repot before all roots are lost, and to encourage new root formation into fresh medium where there is a good chance of survival. Whether it be a result of higher oxygen levels, or a lesser chance of disease attack, orchids with few viable roots (and those with a good number) are generally more inclined to form new roots in a drier medium than one which is wet. After re-stricting water to bring this about, the trick then is to avoid severe desiccation during this tenuous root-deprived period. Provide conditions which discourage high transpi-ration (water loss) rates (such as high hu-midity, lower light intensity) until new roots are formed and on their way toward establishment. Some growers will not pot a rootless orchid until new roots are initiated, keeping the plant in a bag, under a bench, or on a flat of moist medium to achieve these low-transpiration conditions.

It is fairly obvious when a sympodial orchid is about to outgrow its container and will soon need repotting. For monopodial orchids (those which grow vertically), this is not likely to be the reason for repotting. Determining whether repotting is necessary because of media decomposition requires a bit more investigating. Naturally, as media break down and become less porous, they take up less space in the pot. A lowering of the level of a medium is a good indication of decomposition. An examination of any roots along the surface will reveal whether they have declined. Jiggling the plant in its pot will also indicate root condition. Any significant shifting of an established plant suggests substantial root loss. Examining the resistance of the medium with a probing rod or finger is another method of assessing decomposition. If there is little resistance, it is likely major decomposition of the mix has taken place.

How to Repot Assemble supplies before beginning a repotting project. Necessary items: containers, mix, stakes, wire, rhizome clips and sterilized cutting blades. Select a firm surface on which to work. Soak the medium in water prior to repotting. Wear disposable gloves for each plant repotted. Spread newspaper on the work surface or swab the area with Clorox between pottings.

These photographs show how to repot a *Potinara* hybrid (above). This intergeneric hybrid exhibits sympodial growth, which is typical of a cattleya or dendrobium.

Step 1 Remove the plant from its container (above). This is easier to accomplish when the medium is moist. In addition, a moist mix more easily separates from the roots. The roots themselves are perhaps more pliable and less likely to break when moist. If the plant resists removal, a sterilized knife inserted and run along the inside surface of the pot may help to separate the rooted medium from the container's walls.

Step 2 Remove the old medium with care in order to preserve as many viable roots as possible (above). Some living roots will inevitably be broken. After all the mix has been removed, sever damaged and dead roots with sterilized scissors or clippers. This reduces the likelihood of infection.

Groom the plant: remove dried pseudobulb and rhizome sheaths, dead or diseased leaves and pseudobulbs. This is also a good time to decide if the orchid needs dividing. This potinara does need dividing (note vertical line) and could be separated into two divisions. Gently pulling the two pieces apart, and cutting the rhizome with a sterilized knife, yielded two plants (below).

Step 3 Choose a sterilized container of the right size. Do not over-pot orchids. Larger-than-necessary containers, while seemingly providing ample room for new growth and thus a longer time before the next repotting, are counterproductive. Media in such containers last a shorter time than those in smaller pots because they remain wet longer. Drying more slowly, decomposing more quickly, such media are less aerated as well. The great majority of orchid roots avoid the relatively airless and wet interiors of a mix, preferring to grow nearer the interior surface of the pot. This tendency is more pronounced the larger the pot and the greater the amount of mix.

All these tendencies work against, not for, a plant placed in too large a pot. The old rule-of-thumb applies: When repotting, the new pot should be large enough to accommodate no more (and no less) than two years of additional growth. Because few conventional media last any longer than two years at a maximum, there is no point in using a larger pot.

Step 4 To further enhance the all-important drainage and aeration of a mix, whatever the size of the container, layer inert material, such as clay shards, gravel or foam packing chips, in the bottom few inches of the pot before inserting the plant and medium.

Step 5 Position the plant in the pot (above). For horizontally-growing sympodial orchids, the greatest distance between the plant and pot edge should be on the side where new growth is most likely to occur. This is where the space will be needed. With cattleyas, for example, this means placing the oldest pseudobulbs, the backbulbs, flush against the edge of the pot, in turn providing the largest area immediately in front of the most recent growth. Once the plant is in position, its rhizome should be level with, or just below, the top of the pot. Vertically growing monopodial orchids, such as vandas and phalaenopsis, should be placed in the middle of the container. This allows root growth to radiate evenly in all directions from the plant, and aids in plant and pot stability.

Step 6 Add the previously prepared and moistened mix (next page). While holding the plant in position with one hand, scoop in handfuls of mix with the other. When enough has been added to hold the plant in place, press the mix around the roots with both hands. Tap the pot and plant on the potting surface occasionally to fur-

Mounting Orchids Encyclias, cattleyas, sophronitis, *Brassavola nodosa* and *Broughtonia sanguinea* are among the many orchids that can be secured to a slab of tree fern, cork or other mount.

Attach a hook to one end of the support so it may be hung where the orchid will receive adequate ventilation. Tie the orchid in place securely with monofilament or wire. Wrap the line around the slab and plant as many times as necessary, so that the base of the orchid does not move. Occasionally, growers place a small pad of absorbent material, such as sphagnum moss, sheet moss or osmunda, between the plant and the slab to retain moisture around the roots. With proper care, new roots will form and adhere to the mount.

There are several ways to display mounted orchids. Suspend them from individual metal hangers or group them on hardware cloth or chicken wire stretched on a frame.

(Stephen R. Batchelor worked for the American Orchid Society, serving as editorial assistant [1979-1981], assistant editor [1981-1983] and acting executive director/editor [1983-1984].)

ther settle the mix. This ensures that no gaps in the medium will remain, and that the plant is secure. Add additional mix until the medium rises to the level of the rhizome, in the case of sympodial orchids, or well covers the area of greatest root production at the base of most monopodial orchids.

Step 7 The plant should be in its initial position and firmly in place. An orchid that wobbles in the container cannot establish itself properly. Stake tall (monopodial) or top-heavy (sympodial) orchids to provide additional support. Rhizome clips and upright support wires that slip onto the edges of containers contribute support. Fortunately, modern breeding, particularly with the *Cattleya* types, has brought down the height of most hybrids, so that staking for plants in bark mixes, a requisite for the giant hybrids of the past, is no longer usually required.

Step 8 Secure the name tag in the new container.

Step 9 Return the orchid to the growing area, unless many roots were removed. If such is the case, place it in a slightly shaded area where it can recuperate.

Although some shriveling may occur immediately after repotting, when done properly an outburst of new roots should soon result. These new roots should readily penetrate and establish in the fresh medium, enhancing the water and nutrient absorption so crucial for successful growth and flowering.

Sophronitis acuensis 'Bronstein-Walsh', AM/AOS, attached to a plaque. Growers: Howard Bronstein and Bill Walsh.

Raising Healthy Orchids

By James B. Watson

HEALTHY ORCHIDS ARE THE RE-sult of a carefully planned culture regimen in which the plants are observed on a regular basis and grown in a clean environment. Many ailments can be quickly detected and dealth with before they affect other specimens in a collection. A few minutes spent each week checking plants is the best prescription for a clean bill of health.

An effective program begins with the purchase of vigorous orchids. Invest in specimens bearing green leaves devoid of black or yellow marks. The plants should be securely rooted in a mix that is firm, not mushy and acrid.

Isolate new purchases for two weeks before adding them to a collection to prevent any insects or diseases from infecting other orchids. If any ill effects are noticed, take the plant back to the seller and ask for advice, or request a replacement.

Maintain a spotless growing area. Remove faded flowers and dead leaves promptly. Water early enough in the day so the plants and flowers dry by night. Do not let puddles of water accumulate. Operate fans or open windows (during warm weather) to provide adequate ventilation. Fertilize enough, but not too much, or weak growth, that is susceptible to insects and diseases, will result.

When an infection is noticed, act swiftly. Identify the culprit. Take the plant (or a sample leaf or flower) to an orchid society meeting, the nursery where the plant was purchased or a county cooperative extension service. Wrap the sick specimen in a plastic bag to prevent it from infecting plants at the destination. However, do not leave it in an unvented car in the summer, or an unheated car in the winter, or additional injury may result. The ailment will most likely be one of four basic kinds:

Insects   Aphids, scale, mealybugs, thrips and spider mites are a few of the insects that attack orchids. The first three are easily seen; the last pair require the aid of a magnifying lens. Talk with local orchid growers to learn how to identify these insects and their symptoms. New growth and buds are common attack points. Understand the insects' life cycles and apply repeated doses of a control to eliminate all phases.

Disease   Fungi and bacteria injure orchids. A warm and humid environment with inadequate ventilation creates the perfect atmosphere in which fungi and bacteria thrive, causing soft spots, sunken areas on leaves, root rot and other ailments.

Viruses   Orchids are prone to viruses that can cause flowers to be abnormal. Typical symptoms are streaking of color and deformity of flowers, and irregular light and dark streaks in leaves. When uncertain if a virus is to blame, consult a professional. Businesses exist that will test orchids for the presence or absence of virus. Destroy virus-infected plants; viruses can infect other orchids and cause harm. Viruses are spread by animal and insect vectors, and by improper hygiene, such as ineffective sterilization techniques on recycled pots and clips, and cutting tools. When severing a flower cluster or dividing orchids, always sterilize the cutting tool by passing the blade through a flame or dipping in alcohol. Use disposable gloves on each plant to be divided.

Physiological Disorders   An imbalance of water, light and temperature creates symptoms of problems. For example, overwatering can cause roots to rot, and, because the plant cannot absorb water, the pseudobulbs to shrivel. The effect is noticed on the pseudobulbs, but the cause is in the medium. Frequently, a change in the care program will solve physiological ailments.

Once an insect or disease problem is identified, choose an appropriate solution. Do not reach for the nearest available pes-

Inadequate air circulation and damp conditions can induce *Botrytis cinera*, which ruins flowers with its fine speckling.

Soft, cottony mealybugs on this new paphiopedilum growth will deform the leaves. Prompt action is necessary to eliminate the insects.

ticide. Consider effective options that will not harm the environment. A cluster of aphids on a cattleya shoot can be carefully wiped off with a cloth soaked in sudsy warm water. Dab away mealybugs lodged in a bloom sheath with a cotton swab dipped in alcohol. Diatomaceous earth sprinkled on the medium discourages snails and slugs.

Occasionally it is necessary to rely on a chemical, especially when many plants are involved. Some growers plan regular spray programs to control insects and diseases. Houseplant insect sprays are handy to spot-check a single plant, especially in the home (but remove the plant from the growing area prior to spraying); more elaborate systems may be employed for larger operations.

Before spraying, be forewarned that some chemicals will damage flowers. The oil carrier (usually xylene) in emulsifiable pesticides can injure flowers or plants, often in conjunction with high temperatures.

Frequently repeated applications are necessary to eradicate all traces of an insect. Be prepared to spray two or three times at seven- to 10-day intervals.

Before applying any chemical:
• Write down the phone number of a physician or a local poison control center.
• Make sure no people or pets are in the area. Keep them away from the spray site for 24 hours.
• Move orchids grown indoors to a well-ventilated area.
• Read the label directions.
• Make sure the substance is recommended for orchids.
• Be certain the toxin is the right one for the job.
• Wear appropriate clothing to protect yourself.
• Know how to dispose of the unused toxin.
• Clean yourself thoroughly after applying any toxic substance.
• Clean the equipment and then store it beyond the reach of curious hands.
• Make sure the area has been replenished with fresh, clean air before family, friends and pets re-enter the area.

Some orchids benefit from being placed outdoors for the summer. Before their return indoors in the autumn, thoroughly inspect each specimen to prevent any unwanted guests from entering the growing area. Once indoors, populations of aphids, mealybugs, spider mites and other insects increase dramatically in the warm and moist environment. Inspect the container's sides, drain hole, developing buds and all of the foliage, especially the undersides of leaves, where insects often lurk.

Spend the time to understand how orchids grow during each season. Then, should a problem arise, it can be dealt with effectively in a way that is safe for the plant, the owner and the environment.

(*James B. Watson is director of publications at the American Orchid Society.*)

Orchid Ailments

LEAVES

Yellowing leaves — This is a normal aging process if only old leaves on backbulbs are involved. If newer leaves yellow and soften, look for: 1) too much light, 2) low temperature, 3) lack of nitrogen (especially in bark), 4) loss of roots.

Blackened areas on leaves — The sudden appearance of brown then black areas on exposed surface of leaves on a bright, hot day, may be sunburn — check shading; if blackened areas increase in size, it might be bacterial or fungal disease — cut off diseased area, treat with fungicide, isolate plant, and dry it off.

Shriveled pseudobulbs — A sign that the plant is losing water content, it can be caused by: 1) low humidity, 2) underwatering, dry medium, 3) loss of roots.

Blackened tips or ends of leaves — This could be caused by: 1) overfeeding, especially in cymbidiums — cease fertilizing and flush plant thoroughly with plain water, 2) excessive soluble minerals in water — have water analyzed; 3) leaf dieback, a fungal infection — cut off blackened areas and treat with fungicide.

Brown or black streaking or mottling of leaves — This could be a virus infection. Send a leaf to your nearest agricultural experiment station.

Small spots on leaves, reddish brown turning black — Probably a fungus infection favored by warmth, high humidity and poor light — reduce humidity or dry off affected plants and treat them with fungicide.

FLOWERS

Deformed flowers — If deformed flowers are produced each year by a plant, it is probably inherent — destroy the plant. An occasional deformed flower can be caused by: 1) high temperatures and low humidity when buds were developing; 2) mechanical or chemical injury to bud; 3) nonrecurrent and unexplained anomaly in bud development; 4) virus infection — isolate plant.

Rapid wilting of flower — If dorsal sepal wilts or dries early, or entire flower "goes to sleep" shortly after opening, it could be caused by: 1) air pollution by ethylene or other gas; 2) too sudden a change of climate or culture; 3) pollination by an unknown pollinator.

Spotting of flowers — Light brown or pinkish dots and spots on a flower after opening usually indicate fungus, *Botrytis*, or sooty mold — reduce humidity, increase ventilation or air movement, remove spotted and old flowers from greenhouse.

Punctures in flowers — Denotes presence of: 1) aphids, soft-bodied sucking insects, or 2) thrips, small chewing insects.

Bruises on flowers — Either mechanical damage or red spider mites — spray with a miticide.

Chewed or eroded flowers, buds or roots — Shows presence of: 1) slugs or snails — use dust or bait, or 2) cockroaches — use chemical or natural control on ground, on plants and pots.

Color mottling of flowers — This could be a color-breaking virus — isolate plant and get an experienced opinion; destroy the plant if virus is confirmed.

ROOTS

Loss of roots — Numerous causes, difficult to diagnose: 1) overwatering; 2) black rot, an infection of *Pythium ultimum*; 3) slugs or snails; 4) excessive salt content of water; 5) potting medium old and broken down — repot after soaking plant in natriphene solution.

ENTIRE PLANT

White cottony masses or gray, brown, blackish crust on underside of leaves, on flower stem, in axils of leaves, etc. — Mealybugs or one of the many scale insects. Scrub with soft toothbrush dipped in rubbing alcohol.

SELECTIONS

Angraecum
Cattleya
Cattleya Relatives
Cymbidium
Dendrobium
Dendrobium nobile
Dendrobium phalaenopsis
Masdevallia
Miltoniopsis
Odontoglossum
Oncidium
Paphiopedilum
Phalaenopsis
Vanda
Vanda Relatives

■

Encyclopedia of
Less Common Genera

The spider-like flowers of *Brassia* Lance (*caudata* x *gireoudiana*) may reach more than 15 inches in height. Bright light, adequate air circulation and plenty of water develop robust plants.
Grower: Charles Marden Fitch.

Angraecum

By Fred E. Hillerman

ANGRAECUM, AND SOME RELATED genera, are constantly gaining popularity. Collectively, they are called angraecoid orchids. Though lacking the sensational colors of cattleyas, vandas and paphiopedilums, the angraecoids bring to the discerning hobbyist a wealth of exotic forms, spicy scents and the purest of whites, as well as the greenest of greens. And the compact size of many species permits their cultivation beneath lights and on the windowsill. Angraecoids range from 6-foot giants to the tiniest of miniatures. Most, however, are modest in size and are suited to 3- to 6-inch pots or tiny slabs.

Compact growth, pretty white flowers and fragrance add up to a winner in *Angraecum leonis* 'Jenny's Moonbeam', CCM/AOS. Grower: Lawrence Schweitzer, MD.

Angraecoids come mainly from Africa and Madagascar; the latter is home to most of the more showy species. With a large number of species, one would expect them to originate from a wide range of climates, altitudes and latitudes, and such is the case here. Fortunately, those that are most popular and provide the best flowers come mainly from altitudes of 3,000 to 6,000 feet; these are well suited to intermediate greenhouses. A much smaller number of showy species is found at low altitudes and hence are warm growers, but these also do fairly well in intermediate conditions. Fortunately, although many of these species can tolerate quite low temperatures, they also thrive with warm, bright days and do not suffer from an occasional 90 F day in the greenhouse. It is easy to make selections from the nearly 1,000 species that will provide white and green flowers year-round. About 200 species have showy flowers.

The genus *Angraecum* (an-GRY-kum), native mainly to Madagascar, has more than 50 species with showy white flowers ranging in size from 1 to 8 inches wide and, if the nectary is included, up to 18 inches long. (The nectary is a slender tubular spur that projects behind the flower.) Most of these are very white, but a few have green-to-ivory-colored sepals and petals. Many are exotic in shape. *Aeranthes* (ay-er-AN-theez) is characterized by green flowers at the ends of long, thread-like inflorescences which bloom for several months up to several years. Forty species are native to Madagascar and neighboring islands. *Aerangis* (ay-er-AN-gis), with about 60 species, is noted for its long spikes of highly fragrant flowers that give the illusion of a flock of white birds all poised for flight. The 45 species of *Jumellea* (joo-MEL-ee-ah) bear strongly scented, snow-white flowers. These are only a few of the genera of angraecoids orchidists relish.

Temperature and Humidity Most angraecoids grow well with 60- to 80-percent humidity and temperatures of 57 to 85 F. Short periods of temperatures 10

© CHARLES MARDEN FITCH

degrees higher or lower are tolerated with little or no damage. Obviously, those species from warm, tropical climates do best in a warm house, while those from 3,000 to 6,000 feet grow best under intermediate conditions. Only a few, including *Angraecum sororium* and *Angraecum protensum,* require three months of chilling to flower.

Light A few species, such as *Angraecum sororium* and *Angraecum magdalenae,* need high levels of light; most grow and flower reliably in 50- to 75-percent shade, and many flower under very shady conditions. *Angraecum leonis, Angraecum magdalenae* and *Aerangis fastuosa* will grow and flower when cultivated under lights.

Air Movement Reliable air movement in the greenhouse benefits most orchids, angraecoids included. Plants should be moving and swaying, but not thrashing. In the warmer southern states, adequate air movement is especially important.

Watering Provide *Phalaenopsis*-like watering conditions for species with fine roots. Those species with large, aerial roots prefer *Vanda*-like watering conditions. Most angraecoids are quite sensitive to water quality and will eventually decline where high amounts of dissolved salts pollute the water. Species of *Aerangis* especially prefer water with low salt content; if such water cannot be supplied continuously, it is very helpful to dunk the entire plant occasionally in distilled or rain water for 20 or 30 minutes. Where water has less than 100 ppm (parts per million) of salts, this is unnecessary; growers in areas with 300 ppm salts in their water need to be more concerned. Slab culture will suffer with hard water.

Fertilizing Apply 30-10-10 or 20-10-10 year-round: bimonthly during the summer, which is the growing season, and once every four to six weeks in the winter.

Potting Practices that apply to *Cattleya, Phalaenopsis* and *Oncidium* satisfy most angraecoids. There are some species with special requirements. *Aerangis* species do well mounted on slabs if adequately

For many hobbyists, the graceful spur behind numerous angraeoid flowers imparts a touch of whimsy. But in their native habitat, this tubular extension of the flower may play an important role in the reproductive biology of these orchids. Nectar deep in the spur rewards nocturnal moths that visit these flowers and thereby effect pollination. Shown here is *Aerangis articulata* 'Avalanche', AM/AOS, one of many angraecoids that makes a fine addition to any greenhouse collection. Grower: Fred A. Stewart, Inc.

watered and seem to benefit from air circulating around the roots. In the past, culture on slabs or in baskets was stressed; however, experimenting has shown that most *Aerangis* will tolerate potting (in fir bark mix or in New Zealand sphagnum moss), if the mix allows plenty of air movement. A few angraecums come from semi-terrestrial habitats and need finer mixes.

(Fred E. Hillerman owned The Angraecum House in Grass Valley, California.)

Cattleya

By Ned Nash

THE SPECIES AND HYBRIDS OF THE *Cattleya* (KAT-lee-a) Alliance are likely the most popular orchids. Even the most passing acquaintance with this group makes it easy to see why. Dedicated species growers appreciate the vast diversity in sizes and shapes, ranging from tiny *Constantia cipoensis* to the enormous *Schomburgkia tibicinis*. Within *Cattleya*, plants range from the 6-inch-tall *Cattleya luteola* to *Cattleya guttata*, which can be more than 5 feet tall when in flower. More than 100 years of hybridizing in this group has led to a diverse array of shapes, colors and sizes. Add to these desirable traits the relative ease of culture and an adaptability to almost any climatic region, and it becomes clear why cattleyas are considered the ideal beginner's orchid.

While greenhouse conditions suit cattleyas best, development of smaller-growing hybrids permits the windowsill hobbyist to indulge in these rewarding orchids. The compact hybrids, in many cases, have the advantage of a species background that renders them more tolerant of cooler and/or warmer conditions than the more traditional types. Although both longtime hobbyists and the relative newcomers are enjoying the popularity of the trend toward miniaturization, to many growers the word cattleya will always stand for the large, frilly orchid seen in corsages.

Forty-eight species of *Cattleya* are native to the middle elevations of Central and South America. An understanding of their native habitat and the conditions under which they occur is invaluable to elucidating their cultural needs. The majority of this group grow as epiphytes on the forest fringes or high in the canopy where they receive strong but dappled sunlight. Because their thick, fleshy roots are largely exposed, owing to their epiphytic habit, the plants have adapted to alternating wet and dry periods. The pseudobulbs are a hedge against this occasional dryness. Plants receive a mild but constant supply of nutrients from many sources, including leaf detritus and animal droppings that are washed from above by the frequent light rains. The temperature and humidity remain fairly constant both because of the particular climatic regime and because of the mitigating influence of the forest itself.

Emulating these interrelated factors contributes to raising cattleyas successfully. Cattleyas will perform well under a wide range of conditions, so it is up to the grower to develop keen observational skills to determine when the plants are satisfied.

Temperature and Humidity Temperature is related to the light regime under which the plants are grown. In nature, the environment is moderated by the overall influence of the forest. Both gentle air movement and the constantly changing amount of light dictated by the foliar cover contrive to keep air temperatures in the 75 to 85 F range. At night, the foliage tends to keep radiant heat from escaping, creating a mild night temperature around 60 F. This day-night differential is equally essential to the health of cultivated plants. Cattleyas in cultivation need a 10- to 15-degree difference between night and day. This means that an optimum range might be 60 F nights and 75 to 80 F days. Meeting these needs is dictated by geographic location. In many regions, nights may be in the high 60s for weeks on end; in others, the days may never reach 60 F. In these cases, both common sense and pocketbook will dictate keeping the differential in line with the naturally occurring conditions.

Another factor to remember is the plants' background. Many of the dwarf types stem from species with more need for cooler

Cattleyas are epiphytes that grow on the trunks and limbs of trees in their native habitats. *Cattleya skinneri* (opposite) is the national flower of Costa Rica. The cultivar 'Krull-Smith', AM/AOS, is shown here. Easy to grow, *C. skinneri* will rapidly develop into a large and floriferous specimen. However, the flowers, which appear in the spring, last only 10 days to two weeks. Grower: Krull-Smith Orchids.

conditions. A majority of the standard yellow-flowered cattleyas prefer warmer conditions. There are usually microclimates in any growing area where these peculiarities can be accommodated — closer to the heater, nearer the cooler. Young seedlings prefer to be warmer, gradually being moved into normal conditions as they mature.

Adequate humidity is essential. A range from 40- to 60-percent relative humidity is recommended. While relative humidity is naturally inversely proportional to temperature, the reverse is needed by cattleyas. That is, the humidity should rise with the temperature to prevent the plant from being stressed by transpiration. In greenhouses, under-bench misting activated by a humidistat is a practical solution. An alternative is to spray the walks and benches with water. In the home, place plants on a grid over a water-and-gravel-filled tray, or mist them.

Light Cattleyas grow and flower best with strong, dappled sunlight. The most common cause for failure to flower is insufficient light. Growths and flower spikes should develop straight and strong without the need for staking. Foliage should be medium olive green. If the growths are weak and floppy, and the foliage a very dark green, the light is insufficient. Conversely, if the foliage is more on the yellow side and quite hard, the plants may be receiving too much light. While it will flower, the plant is probably being stressed and will not perform to its optimum.

In the home, cattleyas prefer an eastern, western or lightly shaded southern exposure. The smaller-growing hybrids and species are much more satisfactory for the windowsill. Both the dwarf hybrids and younger seedlings can get along with, and indeed generally prefer, lower light than do the larger types.

An important note for those contemplating growing cattleyas in the home — under lights or at the windowsill — is the importance of light quality. Increased quantity — longer hours — of light will not compensate for poor quality light. Overlong day length —

RICHARD CLARK

more than 16 hours — can result in stress symptoms: weak growth, tip burn on the newest growth and failure to bloom.

Watering In nature, the exposed roots of cattleyas enjoy a rather rapid cycle of wetting and drying. Although the bulk of cultivated plants are grown in pots, this wet-dry cycle must be duplicated by allowing the plants to become nearly dry before watering. Most newer growers tend to err on the side of too much water rather than too little. An old saying goes, "When in doubt, don't." However, common sense is again the watchword here. Do not allow pseudobulbs to shrivel from lack of water before any is applied.

There are several good diagnostic techniques for determining the amount of water left in a given pot. When in need of water,

the pot will usually be lightweight. Insert a freshly sharpened pencil into the pot in question. If the point is dry when removed, the plant needs water. A circle of moisture left underneath a pot indicates that the plant is moist enough for the time being. It has been recommended that each plant be individually checked for moisture content before watering. This can be very bothersome and time-consuming. Grouping pots of similar size permits development of an economical watering schedule. In general, mature plants need water no more than once a week. Smaller and younger plants may need it more often, so observe.

Fertilizing The single best piece of advice that can be given about the feeding of cattleyas is to do it "weakly, weekly." Most commercial preparations give instruc-

The term "cattleya" is often casually applied to intergeneric hybrids in the *Cattleya* Alliance, including *Hawkinsara* Toddler 'Show Off', AM/AOS (*Slc.* Pre-School 'Impish' x *Ctna.* Why Not 'Idol's Eye') (opposite above). Grower: Stewart Orchids. An unusual color blend is presented in *Sophrolaeliocattleya* Twinkle Twinkle 'Evening Star', HCC/AOS (*Slc.* Precious Stones x *Cattleya intermedia*) (opposite below). Grower: Stewart Orchids. Clusters of brilliant flowers top the compact-growing *Potinara* Twentyfour Carat 'Solid Gold', HCC/AOS (*Potinara* Lemon Tree x *Brassolaeliocattelya* Yellow Imp) (above). Grower: Jerry Rehfield.

tions to feed every two weeks at a certain rate. Much better results can be obtained by using a dilution of half the recommended rate each week. As can be inferred from their natural habitat, cattleyas are moderate feeders accustomed to a constantly available mild nutrient solution.

The type of fertilizer used is dictated by the particular type of mix in which the plants are potted. There are three basic types of mix: organic, requiring no additional feeding; organic, requiring additional feeding; and inorganic, requiring addition of all nutrients. For many years, cattleyas were potted in osmunda, which required no additional fertilization for the plants to flourish. Fir bark and tree fern exemplify the second type of mix that requires a relatively high ratio of nitrogen. Today, with the harvesting of tree fern regulated and the supply of good-quality fir bark declining, much experimentation is going into essentially inert, inorganic media. Growing in such a mix is similar to hydroponics, in which the fertilizer must supply all necessary ingredients for the plant's growth.

Leach the potting mixture thoroughly every four weeks. Water the plants copiously once and then do it again. This will help to prevent a harmful buildup of salts in the potting mix.

Few flowers generate the enthusiasm shown for the classic *Cattleya*-like flower, typical of those seen in corsages. *Potinara* Catherine Raymer 'Mt. Rainier', HCC/AOS (*Potinara* Tapestry Peak x *Laeliocattleya* Pirate King), makes it easy to see why some orchid growers devote their entire collection to the genus *Cattleya* and its related intergeneric hybrids. Grower: Krull-Smith Orchids.

Potting Repot cattleyas when the mix decomposes or the plant outgrows its container. These events usually occur together at two-year intervals. The mix in which cattleyas are potted should be moderately coarse and freely draining to meet their preference for epiphytic-like conditions.

The question of when to pot a particular plant can be one of the most frustrating for new and experienced growers alike. Do not repot a plant in bud. If such a task must be undertaken to save the plant, remove the buds. Repot when new roots are seen emerging from the base of the newest growth, or ideally just before they are expected. This may be in conjunction with growth initiation, after flowering, or both. Most cattleyas are relatively tolerant of potting any time. Certain species, notably bifoliate cattleyas (such as *Cattleya amethystoglossa*), will not grow unless they are potted when roots are initiated. Pot just before root initiation because the newly emerging roots are quite brittle and sensitive to breakage. If they are carelessly broken before they reach a certain length, that growth may never produce any new roots. For this same reason, it is important to pot the plants firmly, even if they must be staked and tied, so that the new roots are not damaged by the plant rocking in its pot.

The potting mix of choice since the late 1950s has been fir bark. In the last few years, quality has steadily declined as the supply of virgin growth trees has given way to softer-barked second- and third-growth timber. The mix does not last as long. Tree fern is still widely used in the more tropical areas. New Zealand sphagnum moss was hailed as the cure-all medium several years ago, and still does a good job on smaller seedlings in pure-water areas. It has not proven as effective for larger plants in larger pots. Various media utilizing largely inert substances, such as vermiculite, charcoal, perlite, rock and the like, have been advertised and used with varying degrees of success in different environments. What works best for the grower is the best medium for the plants.

Growers who find their mix of choice more difficult to obtain are resorting by necessity to experimentation with new materials. There are several important things to remember with such experiments. First, utilize only less-than-desirable and/or duplicate plants so that an irreplaceable clone is not lost. Second, the plant(s) will take some time to react, either favorably or unfavorably, to any new medium. Give them a chance to adjust. Begin trials only after it is determined the proposed mix is convenient and easy to use; is readily available locally; and is relatively inexpensive.

(Ned Nash is director of conservation at the American Orchid Society.)

ALL PHOTOGRAPHS THIS PAGE: STEPHEN R. RATHCFI OR

Cattleya buds emerging from sheaths that turn brown and necrotic (top). Sometimes it is necessary to slit open the sheath gently to help the buds grow out. When a cattleya develops purple pigmentation in both its leaves and pseudobulbs, it often indicates the plant is receiving too much light (above).

Cattleya Relatives
By Gary Baker

THE *CATTLEYA* Alliance embraces many popular orchids, which require care similar to cattleyas. All of these orchids are native to the New World Tropics and have contributed to the development of numerous hybrids and intergeneric hybrids. *Isabelia* and *Sophronitis* species are ideal for growing under lights. *Brassavola nodosa* and *Rhyncholaelia digbyana* are delightfully fragrant. And laelias and schomburgkias are worthy of consideration by anyone in the tropics wishing to grow orchids on trees. Clearly, the *Cattleya* Alliance offers something for every orchid taste.

Barkeria   Unlike other members of the *Cattleya* Alliance, barkerias (bar-KER-ee-ah) become deciduous in the winter. Hence, they need to be kept rather dry while in that state. They grow better when secured to a piece of cork, tree fern or other mount; cultivating them in pots, even clay ones, can be tricky. Barkerias appreciate warmth and bright light, so place them with cattleyas. *Barkeria cyclotella* bears bright, deep-magenta flowers during the winter, and, like the other species, needs regular watering when in active growth.

Brassavola   *Brassavola* (bra-SAH-vo-la), terete-leaved (round-leaved) relatives of cattleyas, tolerates considerable light and thrives when cultivated with cattleyas. Do not divide too often. They do especially well if mounted on a piece of tree fern or cork, where the stems may ramble and water will drain away from the roots. *Brassavola nodosa*, the wonderfully nocturnally fragrant lady-of-the-night orchid, is typical in preferring a slight drying off when new growths mature. Like the other 15 members of this genus, its flowers are white, pale green or light yellowish.

Broughtonia   *Broughtonia* (brow-TOH-nee-a) *sanguinea*, one of two species in this genus, is native to Jamaica. Its 1-inch flowers are generally crimson or rose-pink, although yellow and white forms are known.

Barkeria scandens is prized for its richly colored magenta flowers. It becomes deciduous in the winter. Grower: Robert Marsh.

Brassavola nodosa 'Saltz', HCC/AOS, emits an aromatic fragrance in the evening. Growers: Mr. and Mrs. Edward S. Wright.

MARK N. WERTHER

© CHARLES MARDEN FITCH

One of Jamaica's gifts to orchid horticulture is *Broughtonia sanguinea,* a rugged little epiphyte with sprays of charming flowers that are typically rose-pink or crimson. Grower: Mark N. Werther.

Cattleya-like flowers in miniature may be viewed on *Isabelia virginalis* 'Fox Den', CBM/AOS. Mount it on a vertical piece of wood or other slab. Grower: H. Phillips Jesup.

The compact plants are best grown on slabs of cork or tree fern (or in small clay pots with perfect drainage). Provide very bright light, keep watering to a minimum and give warm temperatures. However, *Bro. sanguinea* appreciates high humidity, so misting on sunny days is beneficial. These relatives of cattleyas, with their long, occasionally branched inflorescences, will be almost everblooming if conditions are to their liking.

Epidendrum and **Encyclia** More than 1,000 species of *Epidendrum* (eh-pi-DEN-drum) and 150 species of *Encyclia* (en-SIK-lee-ah) offer a bounty of colors and forms, and even fragrance. Basically, the easily grown members of these two genera are treated like most other species of the *Cattleya* Alliance. Certain species, including *Encyclia mariae* and *Encyclia vitellina,* prefer cooler temperatures due to the higher altitudes to which they are native, but most are satisfied with *Cattleya*-like conditions. Many epidendrums and encyclias will grow and thrive under a variety of environments, and species like *Encyclia cochleata,* with its greenish sepals and petals and near-black labellum, will reward hobbyists with masses of striking flowers.

Isabelia *Isabelia* (iz-a-BELL-ee-a) is a delightful, choice miniature whose blos-

soms resemble very tiny *Cattleya* flowers. *Isabelia virginalis* produces mats of pseudobulbs whose fibrous covering makes them look like tiny baskets. The plant's leaves are needle-like, while the diminutive florets are white with a hint of rose. Mount this species on a vertical piece of wood or other slab and keep it quite dry. Good drainage is essential: never allow *Isabelia* to dry out, but never let it become waterlogged either. Provide *Cattleya*-like temperatures and light.

CHUCK MCCARTNEY

Encyclia cochleata hails from Central America, the Caribbean and northern South America. Grower: Mrs. Katherine O. McCartney.

Laelia has contributed to many intergeneric hybrids, including this *Laeliocattleya* Mini Purple 'Debbie Ann', HCC/AOS (*Laelia pumila* x *Cattleya walkeriana*). Grower: Heckeroth Orchids.

Laelia   There are three quite distinct groups of *Laelia* (LAY-lee-a) species. One assemblage encompasses plants which are essentially like standard cattleyas: large, spectacular flowers on plants which look like and require cultural conditions similar to those of the *Cattleya labiata* group. *Laelia purpurata* is typical of this group, its stunning licorice-scented flowers being borne on rampant-growing plants. Treat like a typical cattleya. The second group of species is gathered under the general heading of rupicolous (rock-growing) laelias. These produce small, star-shaped flowers, often in brilliant yellows, oranges or reds, as in the rich yellow of *Laelia flava*. They need superb drainage and can even be grown in shallow clay pots filled with gravel. The third group of laelias, which hails from higher montane regions from Mexico and neighboring countries, tolerates, and often appreciates, relatively cool temperatures. The easily grown *Laelia anceps* can withstand temperatures down to freezing with little or no harm.

Rhyncholaelia   The two members of the genus *Rhyncholaelia* (rink-oh-LAY-lee-a) are far better known under the names *Brassavola digbyana* and *Brassavola glauca*, although they are currently regarded botanically as *Rhyncholaelia digbyana* and *Rhyncholaelia glauca,* respectively. Both have been used extensively in hybridization in the *Cattleya* Alliance, especially *Rhyncholaelia digbyana*, which is responsible for the large glorious lips of *Brassolaeliocattleya* (*Brassavola* x *Laelia* x *Cattleya*). *Rhyncholaelia digbyana* itself possesses one of the orchid world's most remarkable features: an awesome, magnificently fringed labellum. In addition, the species perfumes the night air with a heady citrus fragrance. Culture for these choice orchids is similar to that of cattleyas in

A fringed lip and intoxicating fragrance are trademarks of *Rhyncholaelia digbyana* 'Amado', HCC/AOS. Grower: Dragonstone Orchids.

Schomburgkia features large specimens with tall spikes of attractive flowers, including those borne on *Schomburgkia tibicinis*.

CHARLES MARDEN FITCH

CHARLES MARDEN FITCH

A well-grown *Sophronitis coccinea* 'Ethel Sackett', CCM/AOS, is covered with flowers. Growers: Mr. and Mrs. Joe Sackett.

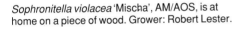

Sophronitella violacea 'Mischa', AM/AOS, is at home on a piece of wood. Grower: Robert Lester.

general, although rhyncholaelias do prefer very bright locations. Keep them under-potted and avoid over-watering. Ample fertilizer enhances development of new growth.

Schomburgkia   Of all members of the *Cattleya* Alliance, *Schomburgkia* (shom-BERG-kee-a) species can tolerate perhaps more direct light than any others. Plants often grow into a rather unwieldy large size, but it is possible to keep them under control if they are divided when repotted. If space is not a limiting factor, members of the genus can become magnificent specimens. Inflorescences can become unusually long in some species, reaching up to 6 feet in *Schomburgkia undulata*. Conditions for standard cattleyas are ideal for schomburgkias.

Sophronitella   The enchanting *Sophronitella violacea*, from eastern Brazil, is closely related to *Sophronitis*. Its cultural needs are similar to those of *Sophronitis*, except that *Sophronitella* (sof-roh-nih-TEL-

ah) prefers warmer temperatures. In this regard, treat it more like a standard cattleya, albeit one that is highly miniaturized.

Sophronitis   *Sophronitis* (sof-roh-NYE-tiss) is a genus of about six species endemic to Brazil that bear brilliant red- and rose-colored flowers. The intense scarlet-red *Sophronitis coccinea* is a most important species in hybridizing, and is in the ancestry of virtually all sophrolae-liocattleyas (*Sophronitis* x *Laelia* x *Cat-tleya*) and potinaras (*Brassavola* x *Cattleya* x *Laelia* x *Sophronitis*). Although related to cattleyas and laelias, cultural requirements of sophronitis are rather distinct from those of these more commonly seen genera. *Sophronitis* needs perfect drainage, constant moisture, high humidity, good light and cold temperatures (nighttime temperatures should be on the low end of cool growing conditions). Pot in a fine compost in small pots or mount them on slabs. Never permit the plants to remain dry for any extended period.

(The late Gary Baker was an AOS judge and wrote for various AOS publications.)

Cymbidium

By James Rose

THE MOST UNIVERSALLY GROWN genus of orchids could be *Cymbidium* (sim-BID-ee-um). Ease of culture, variety of color and lasting quality of the flowers are but a few of the factors that justify its popularity. Although once raised primarily for cut-flower production, cymbidiums today are an integral part of many hobby orchid collections. Cymbidiums are often the first orchid tackled by hobbyists.

The genus consists of approximately 50 species, and many are cool growing. The majority of these originate in the highland regions of India and Burma. Other groups include the miniature species of Japan and China, popular for their small stature; the species of Australia; and species from tropical Malaysia (which are not discussed here because of their great differences in culture). Today's collections consist mainly of hybrids from the first three groups. The group or groups from which these hybrids are derived will dictate which cultural path to follow.

Cymbidiums in the Garden

CYMBIDIUMS MAKE wonderful plants for the home garden in mild frost-free areas. Shelter derived from trees often provides the perfect amount of shading. Do not permit surrounding landscape plants to encroach on the orchids, blocking light or preventing adequate air movement. Check the tree canopy every few weeks to be sure that there is still ample light. Branches will have to be thinned periodically.

Cultivate cymbidiums in mounded beds where the soil has been amended in order to provide proper drainage. Spread bait where snails and slugs pose a threat. Protection against frost may be necessary. Material put over the plants should not touch the leaves. With a little extra care, cymbidiums are an attractive as well as exotic addition to the appropriate garden setting.

Cymbidium hybrids possess tremendous variation in floral color and shape. Flowers are produced on upright or pendulous sprays and can be quite small or quite large. Almost any color except blue is available at nurseries, garden centers, and even supermarkets. Due to the increase in pot-plant production, prices have become competitive, making a favorable marketplace for the consumer. Best of all, cymbidium flowers last longer than almost any other member of the orchid family, with individual flowers remaining fresh for eight to 10 weeks. Though the blooming peak is early spring, it is possible to begin the flower season in October and extend it through June. Indeed, the challenge for many hybridizers is to produce cymbidiums that flower during the summer so that growers can enjoy blooms year-round.

Today's new hybrids address both the disadvantages of growing cymbidiums and providing exciting new styles of flowers. The most common complaint has been that the plants tend to be too large. In answer to this, breeders have improved the quality of miniature cymbidiums and reduced the size of the foliage of standards, which are typically 3 to 4 feet tall. Bright new colors prevail — orange *Cymbidium* Mighty Sunsets (Wyalong Sunset x Mighty Mouse), red *Cymbidium* James Toya (Yowie Flame x Red Beauty) and polychromes (two or three blended colors), such as *Cymbidium* Kiri Te Kanawa (Tamatea x Mighty Mouse), delight collectors. Perhaps even more exciting is a new generation of miniatures, such as white *Cymbidium* Gladys Whitesell (Fifi x *parishii*) and red *Cymbidium* Phar Lap (Flame Hawk x *madidum*) which have commanded attention and awards. Advanced hybrids derived from the green *Cymbidium* Peter Pan (*ensifolium* x Miretta) extend the flowering season, add warmth tolerance and often impart fragrance.

Temperature and Humidity Cymbidiums tolerate considerable temperature variation. Ideal day temperatures are 75 F to 80 F with night temperatures around 50

GORDON FULKS

RICHARD CLARK

Cymbidium Via Nogales 'Pink Cloud', HCC/AOS (Solana Beach x Sussex Dawn) (above left). Grower: Gallup & Stribling. Cymbidium Little Bighorn 'Emerald Meadow', HCC/AOS (Dag x Sussex Moor) (above). Grower: Masako Kawano.

F to 55 F. Strive to keep the heat from exceeding 90 F, but if it does, increase the humidity or invest in a swamp cooler and enclose the collection. A certain amount of warm weather can be dealt with or tolerated during the growing season, but this will often cause developing inflorescences to be deformed or drop their buds. During this time, keep day temperatures under 80 F and nights no lower than 40 F but under 60 F. Cymbidiums will tolerate a few degrees of frost, but temperatures 27 F and below cause damage to the inflorescences. A moderate differential in day/night temperatures of 20 degrees is desirable for the production of quality inflorescences. This can be difficult in areas like South Florida and Hawaii, but there are many new warmth-tolerant hybrids available that grow and bloom in these climates.

Adjust humidity to the season. Provide more than 50 percent during the growing season and less during the flowering season.

Light This is the single most important factor to ensure robust growth and flowers. Inadequate light or sunshine is the most common reason for failure of flowering-size plants to bloom. Provide as much light as possible without burning the leaves. The foliage should have a green, jade-color appearance rather than deep green. Except in rare cases, adequate light cannot be provided to plants grown in the home. Growth will be slower and uneven, and the constant temperature will inhibit inflorescence formation. In parts of the country where the weather in winter is extreme, grow the plants outside during spring and summer, and then move them indoors as late as possible at the first threat of frost. The spikes should be initiated by then and will progress fine under sufficient light, if kept cool. As a general rule, provide 5,000 to 6,000 foot-candles during the growing season and 2,000 to 3,000 foot-candles during the flowering season.

Air Movement Breezy air movement reduces the incidence of disease and invasion of insects. Hot drafts damage the buds, however. Where a space heater is operated at night, distance the inflorescences from the hot air, and provide some humidity.

Long-lasting cymbidiums — including *Cymbidium Rincon Fairy* (Fairy Wand x Rincon) — banish those winter blues with their happy colors.

Watering Water cymbidiums thoroughly to avoid the buildup of fertilizer salts. Cymbidiums are native to monsoon areas, so they require ample water during their summer growing season. This does not mean that during the cool flower season the plants go dormant. Pot size and coarseness of the mix dictate the frequency of watering. A guideline: Water once a week, more frequently during warm weather, and less often in cool or wet weather. Overwatering will cause roots to rot.

Fertilizing The ideal feeding program is dictated by the seasons. Provide a balanced formula (20-20-20) all year long, supplementing with nitrogen in summer, to speed growth. Plants in organic mixes, such as fir bark, require more frequent feeding during the growing season. Apply the fertilizer one-half strength every two weeks rather than once a month. Toward the end of the growing season (June), discontinue the nitrogen supplement to promote the initiation of inflorescences.

Potting Novices are occasionally intimidated by the thought of repotting cymbidiums. Huge plants may fill a 14-inch tub and weigh 50 pounds. A few basic rules simplify the process and transform the challenge into a task that is within the grasp of every grower.

First, do not repot an entire collection at one time. Depending on how overgrown the plant is, the divisions may not bloom the following year. Second, repot them immediately after flowering ceases. This allows the plant sufficient time to develop new growths, form strong pseudobulbs and initiate flower spikes before the next bloom season.

Mix formulas vary from grower to grower. California hobbyists rely on fir bark. One recipe: equal parts fine and medium grade bark with about 15 percent perlite. A porous mix is best as it is always easier to add water than it is to take it away from a sodden medium.

Cymbidium divisions should be a minimum of two to three green bulbs with growths. This size should bloom the next season, providing there is a healthy root system.

Start new plants from turgid backbulbs. Remove all leaves and roots and set in a cool spot until new growth begins to show, then pot. Cut roots on strong divisions back to 6 inches and remove dead roots. Tamp down the mix fairly tightly. The size of the pot should accommodate three years' growth. Provide typical cymbidium conditions once repotting is complete. If divisions are not robust, keep them on the drier side with a little more warmth for a few months.

Reflecting on 100 years of cymbidium growing suggests a bright future. In the approaching century, orchid enthusiasts will have available to them many bright new styles of cymbidiums. Improved plant habit, greater floriferousness and a rainbow of colors will result in compact plants covered with bright flowers lasting many months — truly a living bouquet.

(James Rose is co-owner of Cal-Orchid, Inc. in Santa Barbara, California.)

Propagating Cymbidiums from Backbulbs

WHEN REPOTTING cymbidiums, the problem of what to do with the backbulbs arises. These brown, leafless bulbs are not dead. Dormant vegetative growing points (called "eyes") on the side of each bulb are capable of initiating new growth. Remove a bulb from the clump with a sterile knife or by applying a twisting motion until the bulb breaks free. Strip off the old leaf-sheaths for a clean appearance, taking care not to damage any of the eyes. Label each bulb. Pot a single bulb into a small pot or, if there are several, plant them in a flat. Keep moist and protect from direct sun. Roots will emerge soon after growth begins on the backbulbs. When the new leaves are 6 to 8 inches tall, pot each bulb in a 6-inch pot. Water at the same frequency and fertilize at the same intervals as for mature cymbidiums. Once potted, the bulbs will continue to grow and usually flower within two to three years while still in the original pot.

Step 2   Pot the removed backbulb in its own container or place several in a flat.

Step 1   With an easy twist, a backbulb breaks free from the parent plant. An alternative is to sever the bulb with a knife.

Step 3   With proper light and watering, this backbulb can be expected to flower in two to three years.

ALL PHOTOGRAPHS THIS PAGE: LAURIS H. ROSE

Dendrobium

By H. Phillips Jesup

OF ALL THE TYPES OF ORCHIDS A beginning grower may acquire, dendrobiums will probably be the most challenging to learn to grow and flower. The reason is that the genus *Dendrobium* (den-DROH-bee-um) contains more than 1,000 species and is exceedingly diverse. Botanists divide the genus *Dendrobium* into a number of "sections," each of which comprises a group of more-or-less closely related species that are relatively similar in appearance and in cultural requirements. Therefore, it is very helpful to know which type of *Dendrobium* one has in order to determine its cultural needs. As might be expected, however, there are certain requirements common to nearly all species, which are described here. Specific needs of members of certain sections are presented on page 56.

Popular for its springtime show, *Dendrobium lindleyi* thrives when mounted on cork or wood.

Dendrobiums are found only in the Eastern Hemisphere, from New Zealand north to Japan and westward through Southeast Asia to India and Sri Lanka. In size, they include miniature plants happy in a 2-inch pot set in a lighted plant tray to towering, stately species best grown in a large greenhouse or outdoors in tropical climates.

The flowers range from exceptionally showy to small and insignificant, the latter being primarily of interest to the botanist or horticultural specialist. Virtually every color found in the orchid family occurs in this genus. Flowers of many species combine several colors, with the lips of some bearing blotches of color in striking contrast to the rest of the flower. Some dendrobiums possess exceptionally long-lasting flowers, while those of others are of brief duration. The extremes range from six months for individual flowers in a few cases to less than one day for a handful of species.

The inflorescence is seemingly terminal in some species, the flowers being borne in a loose raceme or dense cluster. Many, however, bear a series of clusters of two or three flowers which emerge from the pseudobulb opposite the leaves.

Some dendrobiums are evergreen; individual leaves will live and function for several years. Others are completely deciduous, dropping all of their leaves upon completion of the current growth. A number of species are partly deciduous, dropping some, but not all, of their leaves annually, at least under most cultural conditions.

Two groups of dendrobiums that have been grown and hybridized extensively — *Dendrobium nobile* and its relatives and the *Dendrobium phalaenopsis* (syn. *Den. bigibbum*) hybrids — are discussed on pages 58-59 and 60-61 in this handbook.

Temperature and Humidity The size and extensive geographic range of this genus have resulted in utilization of natural habitats as diverse as mangrove thickets on the shores of tropical islands, with the orchids growing just above the high-tide level, to mossy limbs in montane cloud

A veritable feast of form and color await those who explore the genus *Dendrobium*. One variation on the theme is *Dendrobium senile* 'Magnifico', HCC/AOS. Grower: Mrs. Ralph Levy.

forests. Of course, each species is found only in the specific habitat in which it evolved. The temperature requirements for each species are keyed to those in which it is found in the wild. To complicate things further, some species grow where there is considerable seasonal fluctuation, with warm, wet monsoon conditions during the summer growth period and cooler, drier winters during which the plants are largely dormant.

Ideal temperatures for those species found in tropical lowlands would be 80 to 85 F during the day and 65 F at night. These temperatures also would be appropriate during the summer for those midelevation species from the monsoon belt. Most of the warm growers do well enough under intermediate temperature conditions in the winter (70 to 75 F days, 60 F nights). Those from the monsoon areas do best in the winter under cool-house conditions (60 to 65 F days, 50 to 55 F nights). High-elevation species from areas where there is less seasonal variation are ideally suited to year-round cool-house temperatures as mentioned above. Their growth cycles also tend to be less seasonal.

A drop in night temperatures to 50 F for at least a month in the late winter induces certain dendrobiums, which bloom at the end of their winter dormancy, to set buds more easily. This includes *Dendrobium nobile* and its hybrids and *Dendrobium kingianum*.

Most dendrobiums, at least when in active growth, do best at a minimum of 50- to 70-percent relative humidity.

Light The majority of dendrobiums grow and flower well under *Cattleya*-like light conditions, which is fairly strong light, amounting to 1,500 to 2,500 foot-candles. As growths mature, it is particularly important to have strong light so that developing pseudobulbs become as large and thick as possible.

Because of their need for light, most dendrobiums are not the easiest orchids to flower under artificial lights or on a windowsill. If they are grown in this way, summering them outdoors with light shade from the midday sun usually is successful in producing strong growths, which are the first requisite for flowering. Give the best light available during the time when they are indoors.

Watering Water dendrobiums copiously when they are in active growth (assuming they are in small pots through which water drains rapidly). Pseudobulbs should be firm and not shriveled while the plant is growing. In warm, sunny weather, a thorough watering every second day is often optimal. The frequency of watering in autumn and winter after growths have matured is a bit more tricky and depends more on the species being grown. Generally, evergreen types should receive just enough water to prevent marked shriveling of the pseudobulbs during this period. But it takes less water to keep them plump than when they are in active growth. Those species that are completely deciduous should receive little water while dormant. It takes only a small amount of water to prevent desiccation for these species.

Fertilizing Large dendrobiums require copious amounts of nutrients when in active growth, when they have vigorous root systems and when they are positioned in strong light. Under these conditions, it is appropriate to apply a dilute solution of a balanced liquid fertilizer such as 18-18-18 (or 30-10-10, if plants are in fir bark) twice a month. The miniature species generally require less frequent fertilizing. Monthly applications when they are in active vegetative growth should be sufficient. When inactive or dormant, dendrobiums require no fertilizing.

Cultivated Sections of the Genus Dendrobium

TO FACILITATE identification and indicate relationships, taxonomists group related species within a genus into sections. Frequently sections also indicate similar cultural requirements. Some of the showier sections of *Dendrobium* with species typical of each are listed here.

Callista (*Den. lindleyi* [syn. *Den. aggregatum*], *Den. densiflorum, Den. farmeri, Den. thyrsiflorum*) — Plants of this group bear dense clusters of yellow, white or lavender flowers in early spring on medium to large plants. These evergreen orchids require cooler temperatures and very little water in winter.

Dendrobium(*Den. aphyllum* [syn. *Den. pierardii*], *Den. anosmum* [syn. *Den. superbum*], *Den. parishii, Den. primulinum*) — The drooping, deciduous canes of these species bear numerous lavender to white flowers in spring. They do best under intermediate temperatures. When these plants naturally drop all their leaves in autumn, give very little water until dormancy ends.

Dendrocoryne(*Den. gracilicaule, Den. kingianum, Den. speciosum*) —These are mostly medium-sized plants, but the group includes some miniatures. Flowers range from white to lavender to greenish. Cool to intermediate temperatures are required along with high light intensities. Keep these species drier than most types year-round.

Formosae [formerly **Nigrohirsutae**](*Den. bellatulum, Den. dearei, Den. formosum, Den. infundibulum*) — These are medium- to dwarf-sized growing species. Nearly all possess white flowers with yellow, orange, green or purple at the base of the lip and black pubescence (hairs) on the leaf sheaths. Most will thrive in intermediate to coolish temperatures, with a moderate dormant period.

Latouria(*Den. atroviolaceum, Den. johnsoniae, Den. macrophyllum, Den. spectabile*) — These medium-to-large plants bear white to greenish flowers marked with violet and green. Grow under intermediate to cool conditions and do not provide a severe rest period.

Oxyglossum(*Den. coerulescens, Den. cuthbertsonii, Den. uncinatum*) — These miniature to medium-sized species from New Guinea bear showy, long-lasting flowers in shades of red, orange, rose-purple and blue. Some require cool conditions, others intermediate. Provide less light than given to other species and keep moist all year. *Dendrobium lawesii* and *Den. cuthbertsonii* (syn. *Den. sophronites*), although in different taxonomic sections, should be grown similarly.

Spatulata [formerly **Ceratobium**](*Den. antennatum, Den. canaliculatum, Den. discolor, Den. gouldii, Den. stratiotes*) — These are the "antelope dendrobiums." Plants are mostly large to very large. Flower segments generally have crisply ruffled margins and the petals often twist to resemble the antlers of antelopes, hence the common name for the group. The blooms are primarily in shades of browns, greens, lavenders, and yellows, and normally are borne in long sprays. Warm temperatures and high illumination are best, with no marked period of dormancy.

Potting Perhaps the single most important aspect of *Dendrobium* culture is proper potting. Almost universally, they do best in a pot very small relative to the size of the plant. They prefer to be pot-bound. The origin of new growths of most species is very close to the previous growth. Therefore, they do not outgrow even a small pot as readily as do cattleyas, for example. This is fortunate because one can use small pots without the necessity of frequent repotting. Dendrobiums resent the disturbance caused by repotting even more than most orchids. The ideal is a container just large enough to accommodate three-to-four years of tightly clustered growths.

The potting medium should reflect the needs of the roots of most species. It should be of rather fine texture, but with perfect drainage. The object of the drainage, which is facilitated by a small pot, is to encourage vigorous rooting so that the medium does not decompose quickly and the plant need not be repotted frequently. This cause-and-effect combination (small pot and fast-draining medium equalling excellent root growth and infrequent repotting) is crucial to cultivate dendrobiums successfully. Because some dendrobiums grow quite tall and others have somewhat arching or pendulous growths, it often is advantageous to hang the small pots to avoid problems of top-heaviness. This is also a good idea from a cultural standpoint because drainage and light are increased to a maximum.

Some of the smaller types of dendrobiums also are grown readily on chunks of tree fern, cork or cut sections of branches. When grown on the latter two, a small pad of sphagnum moss or osmunda fiber placed beneath the plant is useful in preserving moisture for a slightly longer period, particularly if the plants are grown inside the home. *Dendrobium* species that can be grown on mounts are *Den. lindleyi* (syn. *Den. aggregatum*), *Den. cucumerinum*, *Den. cuthbertsonii*, *Den. kingianum*, *Den. lichenastrum* and *Den. linguiforme*.

© CHARLES MARDEN FITCH

An infinite variety of color forms is found in the variable species *Dendrobium cuthbertsonii*, which is sometimes sold under its former name, *Dendrobium sophronites*. The clonal name 'Tangerine', AM/AOS, aptly describes this award-winning plant. Grower: Darrin Norton.

When to repot is as important as how in this genus. The rules applicable to most genera apply here, too, but with even greater emphasis. Most dendrobiums root copiously from new growths when the growths are only a few inches high. By far the best time to repot is when these new roots first appear. The longer repotting beyond this stage is delayed, the greater the danger to the plant. In fact, repotting during relative dormancy after growths have matured can be fatal. Because most dendrobiums begin growths in the spring, this is normally the time to repot.

While dendorbiums can be intolerant of lackadaisical culture, attention to detail is rewarded with an exuberance of handsome flowers. The true enthusiast will as well exult over every new root and leaf.

(*H. Phillips Jesup is a contributing editor of* Orchids *and* Awards Quarterly.)

Dendrobium nobile

By Jiro Yamamoto

DENDROBIUM NOBILE AND RELATED species are native to Burma, India, Thailand and Indochina. Here they grow on trees, from the lowlands up to the cool highlands of the Himalayas at elevations of 4,000 feet. The species and their hybrids are extremely hardy, surviving temperatures ranging from warm to hot as well as enduring freezing conditions in some locales. If kept dry, these species and hybrids will survive winter temperatures of 37 to 39 F and flower around April.

Temperature and Humidity For differentiation of flower buds, it is important to expose plants to low temperatures. The pseudobulbs, which grow from spring through summer and mature in the autumn, require approximately one month of low night temperatures. Therefore, in the autumn when it becomes cool, do not rush to bring plants into the greenhouse, unless a freeze is forecast. Leave them outside to cool, and they will bloom better.

When in full bloom, flowers will last longer if the plant is placed in a cool, dry spot away from any draft and out of direct sunlight. A night temperature of 40 to 50 F is ideal. Water the plant enough to moisten the surface of the medium once every five to seven days during the warmest part of the day. The medium should dry before evening.

Light Small plants require no shade during the winter. However, 30- to 40-percent shade is needed from late spring through autumn for healthy growth. Medium- or flowering-size plants do not need shade any time (unless the leaves begin to burn). Full sun promotes vigorous growth.

Where summer breezes are minimal, provide 30- to 40-percent shade during those months. If ventilation is inadequate in the greenhouse during the flowering season, buds will be damaged, and flowering will be poor. Therefore, 30- to 40-percent shade is recommended from the time flower buds appear until the end of the flowering season.

Watering When temperatures begin to rise in the spring, gradually start watering. In the summer, when temperatures are high and sunlight is strong, water almost every day to keep the plant from dehydrating. In late September, when temperatures begin to fall, gradually reduce watering. When the night temperature falls below 50 F, water only enough to keep the canes from shriveling; once a week should be adequate. When night temperatures fall below 40 F, keep the plants dry. In a greenhouse in which night temperatures are kept above 60 F, water lightly when the plants are dry. It is important that the medium surface is dry by evening.

Fertilizing A low-nitrogen fertilizer is ideal for flowering specimens. Discontinue fertilizing after early August to guarantee many flowers. For small plants grown without supplemental heat, and where night temperatures fall below 45 F in winter, apply fertilizer high in nitrogen when night temperatures rise to about 50 F (March or April). If night temperatures in winter are above 50 F, fertilize in January. The easiest way to fertilize small plants is with timed-release fertilizers that are effective for more than six months. Do not use timed-release fertilizers on flowering-size plants; they may cause over-fertilization.

Inducing Flowers

POOR FLOWERING, in spite of robust growth, and the appearance of keikis are the most common problems with *nobile*-type dendrobiums. The solution: Provide plenty of light to flowering-size plants. As long as there is constant air circulation, they can be grown without shade, even in summer. In Hawaii, plants are grown in full sun (no shading) successfully. If air circulation is inadequate, about 30- to 40-percent shade should be provided in July and August to prevent leaf burn. From September forward, situate plants in full sun to produce strong canes and leaves, and to prepare them for flowering.

Potting Tree-fern fiber, osmunda, fir bark, sphagnum moss and other media appropriate for cattleyas are suitable for *nobile*-type dendrobiums. A mixture of three parts perlite, one part vermiculite and one part peat moss is suitable. A slightly acid medium (pH 5) through which water drains rapidly but still retains some moisture is suggested.

Clay pots are recommended for sphagnum moss or media that retain moisture. For more-porous media, choose plastic or polyethylene containers. Appropriate pot sizes:

• Small plant up to 3 inches tall: use a 2^{1}/$_{2}$-inch pot.

• For a 5-inch-tall plant: use a 3-inch pot.

• For a 10-inch-tall plant: use a 4-inch pot.

Overpotting does not enhance the growth of small plants.

When the night temperatures remain above 55 F, repot overgrown or large plants that have finished flowering. Postpone transplanting when lower temperatures prevail. To repot, remove decayed potting medium and discolored black or decayed roots by washing them with water. Be careful not to damage the live roots. Repot into a container one size larger than the present vessel. If the root-ball's size has decreased due to removal of decayed roots, set the plant into a smaller container.

Plants with more than seven or eight pseudobulbs can be divided, although this is not necessary. Dividing healthy plants with only four or five psuedobulbs hinders the following year's growth. Transplant small or medium-size plants that have finished flowering only when the pot has become too small to support the height of the canes. The best time for planting or transplanting is when new shoots are 4 to 6 inches tall; the new roots from the new shoots will rapidly anchor themselves in the potting media. Do not repot when no new shoots are growing or the plant has stopped growing.

After repotting, keep the medium relatively dry for two weeks. Water once every

YAMAMOTO DENDROBIUMS

Masses of elegant flowers cloak the stems of *nobile*-type dendrobiums in a flurry of color. *Dendrobium* Pink Beauty 'Queen' (Super Star x Lovely Virgin) flowers in the winter and spring.

three to four days, just enough to moisten the surface of the medium. When new roots appear, provide ample water that drains through the bottom of the pot. Keep the plants in 40-percent shade for three weeks after transplanting.

From spring to early summer, keikis (offshoots) may appear on the upper nodes of the pseudobulbs due to damage of the new shoot or because of excessive nitrogen. Keikis produced in the spring produce thick pseudobulbs and mature during the summer. When the roots are 3 to 3^{1}/$_{2}$ inches long, remove the keiki. Soak the keiki in water to soften the roots, then plant in a 3-inch (or larger) pot, depending on the keiki's size. If shoots near the bottom of the pseudobulbs and keikis appear simultaneously, pluck off keikis to encourage development of the main shoots.

(Jiro Yamamoto is owner of Yamamoto Dendrobiums in Mountain View, Hawaii.)

Dendrobium phalaenopsis

By Bob Davidson

PHALAENOPSIS-TYPE DENDRO-bium hybrids are derived from *Dendrobium phalaenopsis* (syn. *Dendrobium bigibbum*). Commonly referred to as den-phals, they are among the easiest of orchids to grow under most conditions. These evergreen orchids reward the beginner with sprays of vividly colored long-lasting flowers in exchange for minimal care.

Arching inflorescences are borne on upright, cylindrical, 2- to 4-feet-tall pseudobulbs, which are slightly swollen at or above the middle. New growths develop from "eyes" near the base of the pseudobulbs and sometimes higher near the leaf joints. Somewhat-leathery, 3- to 6-inch-long leaves clothe the upper half of the pseudobulbs, and usually remain for one to two years. The number of flowers borne on an inflorescence increases as the plant matures. First-bloom seedlings often bear one to five flowers per spray; mature plants can produce 20 or more flowers per cane on each of many canes. Individual flowers last six to eight weeks and provide color for several months each autumn. Den-phal flowers, typically round and flat, with overlapping petals and sepals, range in color from pure white to deep plum and shades and hues in between. To prevent distorting the flowers' orientation, avoid moving or turning specimens once inflorescences begin to emerge.

Trends in breeding of *phalaenopsis*-type dendrobiums have focused on improving flower size and shape, especially among the darker varieties, and developing shorter varieties. Combining traditional den-phals with antelope-type species has led to new colors, larger flowers and an extended blooming season. Some popular intermediate *phalaenopsis*-type *Dendrobium* hybrids: Ekapol (Lim Hepa x Tomie Drake), Sonia (Caeser x Tomie Drake) and Jaquelyn Thomas (*gouldii* x *phalaenopsis*). Intermediate types, carrying flowers in shades of yellow, blue and brown, are especially popular.

Temperature and Humidity Den-phals thrive under a broad spectrum of temperature and light combinations. The recommended temperature range is between 50 and 90 F, but temperatures a few degrees higher or lower are acceptable and produce no detrimental effects. A relative humidity of 50 to 60 percent is optimal. In climates with lower humidity, mist the plants on hot, dry days. Avoid excessive water on the leaves and in the crown of the plants during humid and cool weather to prevent crown rot and fungal problems. Fans which keep the air moving without causing excessive chilling or drying keep the foliage dry, and also help remove heat from the leaves during hot weather.

Light Direct filtered sun is essential for flowering, but provide 30- to 70-percent shade during midday. Bright light will generally encourage flowering, provided excessive leaf temperatures are avoided. Although *phalaenopsis*-type dendrobiums can be grown under artificial lighting, this practice is not recommended due to the plants' height.

Watering The moisture needs of these orchids are similar to those of cattleyas. Thoroughly soak the potting medium, then allow it to dry out before watering again. Watering twice a week is generally adequate with properly potted plants in most climates. In winter, watering frequency may be reduced if the plants take longer to dry.

Fertilizing Apply a balanced fertilizer containing minor elements on a regular basis. When using inorganic media it is especially important to provide an adequate mix of nutrients, including minor nutritional elements. This is important since little nutrition is provided by the decomposition of the potting medium. Avoid high-nitrogen fertilizers (such as 30-10-10), since they encourage the growth of algae and pathogens, and promote excessive leaf growth rather than the development of roots

and flowers. Feed with every watering at half the dilution prescribed on the label. This will guarantee adequate nutrition while avoiding any chance of damaging root tips from excessive nitrogen.

Potting Leave many dendrobiums, and these hybrids in particular, undisturbed in relatively small pots. Provide air circulation around the roots. Choose a potting material which will not decompose quickly. Mixtures of fir bark and inorganic material (lava-rock) have yielded positive results. The inorganic materials impart a porosity to the mix, which permits air circulation around the roots. This mixture allows three years to lapse between repotting efforts. It is important, though, to avoid over-potting, because this slows growth and reduces flowering significantly.

Phalaenopsis-type dendrobiums are particularly suited to hanging in the greenhouse and windows. Clay pots with slits or extra holes are preferred in humid environments, while plastic pots with extra holes are adequate for drier climates. When repotting, avoid planting the growths too

Phalaenopsis-type dendrobium hybrids bear arching inflorescences clothed with delicately colored flowers. One pseudobulb may develop several inflorescences over a number of years. *Dendrobium* Tsuruyo Kamemoto 'Splendor', AM/AOS (Sean Oshiro x *phalaenopsis*), captures the spirit of these magnificent orchids. Grower: Kazuo Kamemoto.

deeply in the mix since the "eyes," from which new growths emerge, will rot easily if covered with mix.

When kept in a pot too long, or another misfortune is experienced, these dendrobiums tend to develop keikis (plantlets) from dormant eyes located near the top of the plant. Once the keikis have grown leaves and fully developed root systems, remove them and pot separately. They will grow into duplicates of the original plant. Development of keikis on a dendrobium is generally an indication that there is a problem with the parent plant which will, more often than not, die soon after the keikis have developed.

(*Bob Davidson owns Davidson Orchids in Palmetto, Florida.*)

Masdevallia

By Marguerite Webb

THE GENUS *MASDEVALLIA* (maz-de-VAL-lee-a) is enjoying renewed popularity. Avidly sought by the Victorians in the middle to late 1800s, masdevallias are once again in the spotlight. This was stimulated by the discovery of new species since the early 1980s and by the production of lovely new *Masdevallia* hybrids. Approximately 500 species and 655 registered hybrids entice hobbyists. A startling array of exotic and whimsical flowers are colored vibrant-to-subtle hues. The tufted plants range in height from 1 to 12 inches, but the majority are compact, affording the grower maximum use of limited space.

Two Spanish botanists, Ruiz and Pavón, described the genus about 200 years ago after they found *Masdevallia uniflora* in the mountains of Peru. They dedicated their discovery to a friend and fellow botanist, Dr. José Masdevall.

Masdevallias are distributed from southern Mexico to southern Brazil, with the greatest concentration in the Andean cloud forests of Colombia, Ecuador and Peru. They occupy a surprising range of elevations, with species occurring from sea level to about 13,200 feet. Masdevallias are epiphytes without pseudobulbs and usually grow on mossy branches or trunks on the shaded lower parts of trees. These cloud-forest inhabitants are frequently bathed in moisture and dried by soft breezes. Although some of the high-elevation species require a cool environment, the majority of the species occur at a moderate elevation of about 6,000 to 6,500 feet and tolerate greater diversity in temperatures.

Masdevallia is the showiest and most popular genus in the subtribe Pleurothallidinae, which also includes the genera *Pleurothallis* and *Dracula*. The sepals are the most conspicuous and most diverse part of the flower; they are usually fused to some degree to form an open cup or occasionally a tube. The apices, or sepaline tails (caudae), are often elongated and are responsible for creating the characteristic appearance of a *Masdevallia* flower.

Temperature and Humidity The need for cool temperatures is the primary reason masdevallias are sometimes considered difficult. But many of the species and the majority of the hybrids respond positively to intermediate conditions. Temperature guidelines:

• Warm growers: winter night — 55 to 65 F; summer day — 75 to 85 F.

• Intermediate growers: winter night — 51 to 60 F; summer day — 70 to 80 F.

• Cool growers; winter night — 50 to 55 F; summer day — 65 to 78 F.

Masdevallias need a minimum 10- to 15-degree differential between day and night. This drop at night is important in the summer. Provide a substantially lower night temperature to minimize heat stress from temperatures in excess of maximum recommendations. High humidity (nearly 100 percent) also helps offset the ill effects of hot summer days. Relative humidity should rise with the temperature.

Because masdevallias are cloud-forest inhabitants, a relative humidity ranging from a minimum of 70 percent to nearly 100 percent is recommended.

Air Movement Air movement is important in the culture of all orchids but, because of temperature and humidity requirements, it is particularly vital in effective masdevallia culture. Adequate air movement reduces leaf temperature, aids in evaporation (thus increasing humidity), and helps reduce the likelihood of fungal and bacterial problems. The air movement should be strong enough to provide a fresh atmosphere, allow for drying of potting media and leaves, and help maintain an even temperature.

Light Masdevallias usually grow in relatively shaded areas in the forest. In cultivation, about 1,000 to 1,400 foot-candles of light is adequate. The leaf color should be medium to light green. Too much light quickly produces yellow leaves; too

little light will result in dark green elongated foliage and poor flowering. Many masdevallias will fit on the windowsill or under lights.

Watering Because masdevallias are relatively small plants potted in small pots, it is necessary to water often. Frequency depends on time of year and type of container and medium, usually ranging from two to three times a week in the summer to about once a week in the winter. Keep the medium moist but not sopping wet. Flush water through pots to ensure thorough wetting. Overwatering does not make up for lack of humidity and will cause root rot.

Fertilizing Masdevallias are not heavy feeders. Apply one-half strength of a balanced fertilizer once or twice a month. Overfeeding may cause leaf-tip burn.

Potting Choice of potting media is a matter of grower preference and dependent on cultural conditions. Masdevallias need a mix that is free-draining yet moisture retentive. Mixtures containing fine fir bark, medium-grade tree fern, osmunda and/or New Zealand sphagnum moss are widely used. Plastic pots retain the moisture in the potting medium longer than clay pots and,

Masdevallia Confetti (*strobelii* x *glandulosa*) is one of several floriferous scented masdevallia hybrids that will grow in warm temperatures.

for that reason, plastic is often preferred.

Repot masdevallias when the potting mix begins to deteriorate, or about every two years. Early spring is the ideal time for repotting because plants re-establish quickly before the onslaught of summer heat. It is best not to disturb masdevallias during the summer. Pot masdevallias so the plants will not wobble when watered. It is important that the crown of the plant is positioned level or slightly above the surface of the media, never below.

Some masdevallias have a pendent inflorescence or climbing growth habits. Mount these on a slab. Tree fern is probably the best support; it will retain some moisture. Place a cushion of osmunda or New Zealand sphagnum moss around the roots and tie the plants in position with monofilament or a similar thread. Mounted plants require more frequent watering, perhaps once a day.

(Marguerite Webb is a co-owner of J & L Orchids in Easton, Connecticut.)

Miltoniopsis

By James Riopelle

IMITATION MAY BE THE SINCEREST form of flattery, but the pansy orchids have achieved for themselves a beauty and charm surpassing that of their namesake. *Miltoniopsis* is a genus of perhaps six species, mostly native to Colombia, which was once lumped into *Miltonia*. Three species of pansy orchids are responsible for all present-day hybrids in this genus: *Miltoniopsis vexillaria, Miltoniopsis roezlii* and *Miltoniopsis phalaenopsis*. These three species are still frequently called miltonias by many orchid growers.

The major blooming season extends from spring to autumn. However, some species and hybrids may flower at other times of the year. The attractive plants are of moderate size, of sympodial growth, with thin, light green leaves, one of which crowns each growing pseudobulb. The lanceolate leaves fan up from the base of the narrow edges of the mature pseudobulbs. From within the snug inner fold of a maturing basal leaf, the inflorescence emerges as a slender, tender, budding growth to produce an arching or drooping spray of two to 10 large, flat, colorful pansy-like flowers. Although fragile looking, these lovely flowers last from 15 to 60 days on the plant; unfortunately their use as cut flowers is limited.

Temperature and Humidity While miltoniopsis will tolerate temperatures of 90 F and above for short periods, keep day temperatures below 80 F by either increasing the shading or providing evaporative cooling. Night temperatures of 55 to 60 F are optimal. The humidity should be moderate when the temperature is low and fairly high when the temperature is high. A humidity range from 50 to 70 percent, such as that given for cattleyas and phalaenopsis, is highly recommended.

Light Pansy orchids require about 1,000 to 1,500 foot-candles of diffused light and will grow well in the vicinity of mottled-leaved paphiopedilums. One alternative is to the side of a south-facing window, protected by shading. Another is to one side of fluorescent lights, perferably next to a cool wall. Increase shading when the temperatures exceed 80 F. Miltoniopsis

---

The Genus Miltonia

APPROXIMATELY 10 species and several natural hybrids comprise the genus *Miltonia* (mil-TOH-nee-a). Most are distributed from central to southern Brazil, and for this reason are frequently referred to as Brazilian miltonias. Flowers may be borne singly, as in the spectacular, aptly named *Miltonia spectabilis* (white, blush, or rich purple), or on spikes, as in the spidery, straw-colored *Miltonia flavescens*. One appreciated feature of miltonias is their habit of having their peak flowering in the summer, when there is a paucity of orchids in bloom. Miltonias can normally be used as cut flowers.

Miltonias are easily grown and notably free-flowering. While they can be grown successfully with pansy orchids, they tolerate wider ranges of temperatures and more light than do miltoniopsis. They thrive on copious watering. Much like pansy orchids, they need a fine compost, through which water drains rapidly, and regular applications of a dilute fertilizer. Their foliage tends to be yellowish-green, but when the leaves become quite yellow, this indicates the plants are receiving too much light.

Miltonias mostly have elongated rhizomes between the pseudobulbs, causing the plants to be rampant growers. Single pseudobulbs of miltonias generally will grow and reach flowering size relatively quickly. Nevertheless, it is not advised to divide plants into small pieces. Because of their rapacious growth habits, miltonias are particularly well suited for growing on slabs of wood, cork or tree fern, where they quickly grow into magnificent free-flowering specimens. — *Gary Baker*

leaves should be light green or light bluish green. If the leaves are dark green, increase light. If the leaves turn yellowish green, increasing shading, Slightly pink leaves indicate maximum acceptable light. Red leaves are a sign of too much light.

Air Movement Brisk air movement of mild air is beneficial to all miltoniopsis. Avoid hot and cold drafts.

Watering The watering demands of pansy orchids are similar to those of thin-leaved cymbidiums. Keep them moist at all times. Inadequate water will cause leaves on new growths to crinkle in accordion-pleated fashion. However, do not let the containers stand in water. During warm weather, and bright winter days in the greenhouse, pansy orchids may require watering daily. When the humidity falls below 30 percent, mist the foliage so that leaves will dry before sunset.

Fertilizing In osmunda, a very dilute solution of an 18-18-18 water-soluble fertilizer used monthly at the rate of ¹/₄ teaspoon per gallon during the growing season is sufficient. Miltoniopsis are moderate feeders, and osmunda supplies some nutrients. In fir bark culture, administer 30-10-10 fertilizer weekly at the rate ¹/₂ teaspoon per gallon of water. Alternate with a lower nitrogen formulation (10-30-20) every fourth application. Because pansy orchids are not deciduous, continue to feed them during the winter at the rate of ¹/₄ teaspoon per gallon, but only if the plants need water. Use a well-balanced water-soluble fertilizer incorporating desirable micronutrients (beneficial trace elements including iron and magnesium).

Potting Pansy orchids are cultivated in many ways using a wide variety of potting composts and containers. Whatever medium is chosen, it should retain some moisture and at the same time permit water to drain away quickly. Do not allow the medium to become sodden. Osmunda, with or without sphagnum, was once considered the best potting medium for miltoniopsis. Since osmunda has become

JULIUS KLEHM

Typical pansy orchid flowers are borne by *Miltoniopsis* Arnold Linsman 'Kansas Red', AM/ AOS (Andy Easton x Leo Holguin), one of many hybrids in this genus enjoyed for their compact size and brilliant colors. Grower: Max Thompson.

less available and more expensive, fir bark mixed with sphagnum (to retain moisture) and perlite or other granular material (to assure drainage), is now quite popular and satisfactory. Add a bit of horticultural charcoal (not from the barbecue) to "sweeten" the mix. To make a bark compost, blend three parts perlite, three parts #4 charcoal, two parts sphagnum (peat) moss and one part cracked oyster shell, with 16 parts of fine fir bark. Recently potted pansy orchids benefit from a top-dressing of live sphagnum moss. A few granules of snail bait (metaldehyde) will control bush snails.

Pansy orchids resent being potted in excessively large containers. Keep them pot-bound. Divide miltoniopsis when the new growing cycle begins. Accomplished growers may divide them at any time. Do not break up the tightly clustered pseudobulbs into divisions of less than three or four growths. Individual backbulbs do not propagate readily.

(The late James Riopelle was a judge emeritus of the American Orchid Society.)

Odontoglossum

By Wally Thomas and Barbara Thomas

FEW LOVELIER SIGHTS EXIST THAN a spray of lacy multihued odontoglossums arching out from the lush green foliage. About 175 species of *Odontoglossum* (o-don-toh-GLOSS-um) hail from the high, cool elevations of the Andes. Closely related genera, with similar cultural needs, occur in Mexico, and Central and South America. Consequently, these orchids thrive and are most popular in those areas that can most easily provide cool moist growing conditions.

A number of intergeneric hybrids involving odontoglossum have been created. These combine *Odontoglossum* with such genera as *Brassia* (*Odontobrassia*), *Miltonia* (*Odontonia*), *Cochlioda* (*Odontioda*) and *Oncidium* (*Odontocidium*). Often these hybrids produce flowers closely resembling the shapes and colors seen in odontoglossums, yet the plants will thrive under much warmer conditions than will purebred odontoglossums.

Odontoglossums, similar in habit to miltonias, are sympodial: bright green leaves arise from oval-and-somewhat-flattened pseudobulbs. The main inflorescence emerges from under the protection of the largest basal side leaf. A second spike may come from the other side of the pseudobulb. There are usually eight to 15 flowers along the inflorescence, which may branch on species cultivated under ideal conditions. Late autumn and spring are the main blooming times, but hybrids may flower year-round. The blooms remain on the plants for several weeks, and, when cut and floated in a shallow bowl of water, last particularly well.

Temperature and Humidity Night temperatures of 52 to 55 F and day temperatures of 65 to 70 F are ideal. However, plants in prime condition will tolerate a wider range, from a low of 45 F to a high of 90 F, for several days. High temperatures tend to prevent the flowers from opening properly, particularly the lip of *Odontoglossum crispum*. Evaporative coolers installed in greenhouses in warm climates increase the chances of raising odontoglossums successfully.

To maintain cool and humid conditions in the greenhouse, water under the benches most mornings and, on bright days, water the leaves (but just enough so that they will be dry by nightfall). This scheme is one way to prevent red spider mites, a microscopic culprit that damages foliage and flowers.

A humidity of 65 percent is ideal, but odontoglossums are surprisingly tolerant of moderately lower or higher levels.

Light Odontoglossums require between 1,500 and 2,000 foot-candles of light. The maximum light permissible results in faint red streaks in the leaves. They may be raised in maximum light, which results in improved flower substance, when provided with cool temperatures and plenty of air movement. In the house, an east-facing window is best. During the frost-free months, set odontoglossums outside in a breezy spot with full open light but no direct sunlight.

Air Movement Odontoglossums thrive in an atmosphere that is fresh and buoyant from the use of fans, ventilation and misting.

Watering The frequency of watering depends on the potting mix and ventilation. Odontoglossums require lots of moisture when rooted in a free-draining mix, but expect decreased vigor if the mix is allowed to remain soggy. Periodically, collect rain water and use it to rinse fertilizer salts that accumulate in the mix. Excess fertilizer causes leaf tips to brown.

Fertilizing Nourish odontoglossums in bark mixes with 20-20-20 fertilizer diluted to one-quarter to one-half of the recommended strength. However, this fertilizer contains neither calcium, magnesium nor sulfur, making it necessary to add these elements where water is soft. Fertilize three of every four waterings, then apply plain water the fourth time.

Odontoglossums put forth sprays of long-lasting flowers boasting lovely colors and unique patterns. Odontoglossum Anneliese Rothenberger 'Gloria R. Weltz', AM/AOS (bictoniense x Goldrausch), is one of many eye-catching hybrids. Grower: S. Robert Weltz Jr.

Potting Bark mixes continue to be the standard potting media for odontoglossums. One mix consists of one part coarse sand, one part coarse shredded peat, one part perlite and four parts fine bark. When an 8-inch pot is used as the measuring cup for these ingredients, add a small handful each of bone meal and dolomitic lime to the total.

Begin with the mix employed by the successful growers of local orchid societies. Repot specimens raised in bark every 12 to 18 months, before the chips decompose, stay too wet and possibly harm the health of the roots. The best time to repot is when the new growth emerges after flowering, which is mainly in the spring but sometimes in the fall. Once beyond the seedling stage, it is essential that the rhizome be cut and examined for rot, which

appears as black and/or reddish areas. Flame sterilize the cutting tool — pruning shears, a knife or single-edged razor blade — between cuts. When clear white shows in the rhizome, flame the broad blade of the shears and hold it against the raw surface to sear it closed. Remove old shriveled bulbs and any dead or unhealthy roots. Invert a small pot in the center bottom of the pot in which the odontoglossum will be planted. Hold the plant so that the base of the rhizome is about $^1/_2$ inch below the rim of the outer pot. Position the plant so that there is room for at least one new growth in front. Ladle in the mix, jiggling the larger pot between handfuls. Fill the pot to the rim; the pseudobulbs should be slightly buried. Thoroughly soak the medium after 24 hours.

Odontoglossums can be grown with great success in rockwool. One successful mix is 90 percent medium grade absorbent rockwool and 10 percent perlite. Fill the container so the medium remains loose around the roots (but not so the plant moves around in the container).

Another alternative is perlite, which has been soaked in a tub to get rid of the fine dust. Position the plant in the container and fill the vessel with perlite. Then spread a $^1/_2$-inch-thick layer of pea gravel over the inert medium. The Kord 8-inch saucerless baskets are excellent for this technique, because they provide a reservoir for bottom feeding through capillary action. They are particularly suitable for windowsill growing. It is easy to pot in perlite and repotting is required only when the plant outgrows the container. Most importantly, over-watering is unlikely. When experimenting with rockwool and perlite, try only a few plants for the first six months. Hydroponic complete fertilizer management is required (but not difficult) and the results are outstanding.

(*Wally Thomas, a retired physician living in British Columbia, has specialized in odontoglossums since the mid-1980s. Barbara Thomas holds a PhD in Forest Genetics and Eco Physiology.*)

Oncidium

By H. Phillips Jesup

A GENUS THAT INCLUDES A GREAT many species attractive and intriguing to the hobbyist is *Oncidium* (on-SID-ee-um). The lip dominates the flowers of many oncidiums and, in a number of species, fancifully resembles a full, swirling skirt, with the other, smaller segments being the "dancer's" arms and head. This accounts for this group's popular name, dancing-lady orchids.

Oncidiums are found exclusively in the New World Tropics, ranging from Florida and Mexico through Central and much of South America. The genus contains approximately 600 species and, as with most sizable aggregations, is divided into a number of taxonomic sections of closely related species. The most common flower colors are combinations of yellow and brown, although lavender and white are occasionally seen in the genus. A veritable rainbow of colors is found in the popular variegata oncidiums (now placed in the genus *Tolumnia*). These species and their numerous hybrids are also commonly termed equitant oncidiums.

The individual flowers of many species are not large, but this is more than compensated for in most species by the great numbers of flowers produced on long, often branched inflorescences, producing a shower-of-gold effect. The flowers of some species are used in corsages or as boutonnieres, and the airy sprays of others make handsome floral arrangements.

The flower forms tend to be stylized, the sepals and petals in some crisped and ruffled and with a lacquer-like texture. A diagnostic feature of the flowers is an often-ornate, complicated callus or crest at the base of the lip. This can range from a toothed protuberance to a shiny, warty one. In fact, the genus takes its name from this feature, *Oncidium* being derived from the Greek word *oykos* which means warty and refers to the wartlike growths on the lip. Naturally, this feature (as well as most aspects of flower form) serves a function related to pollination.

Plant forms in the genus vary widely. The majority of species have rather prominent pseudobulbs and strap-shaped, somewhat-thin leaves. One group has terete (pencil-shaped) leaves, whereas another has dwarf fans of hard, three-edged leaves. Plants of another popular group, commonly

The Genus Tolumnia

THE EQUITANT oncidiums — with miniature fans of hard leaves and colorful flowers in combinations of lavender, white, yellow, red and purple — are placed by some taxonomists into *Tolumnia*. This includes *T. guianensis, T. pulchella, T. triquetra* and *T. variegata*. Many hybrids in this group are popular. However, outside of the sun belt, these are not for beginners. Cultivate these in small pots or mount them on pieces of wood or cork. The plants require plenty of water but must have perfect drainage as well. They prefer *Cattleya*-like light conditions and temperatures.

Oncidium Native Dancer 'Sundance', HCC/AOS (Classy 'Island Dancer' x *desertorum*).

ANITA ALDRICH

called the mule-ear orchids, produce folded, leathery leaves. Inflorescences are produced from the base of the plant in the axils of the sheathing leaves, not at the apices (tops) of the growths as in cattleyas. The inflorescences range from a few inches in length to an extreme of 12 to 15 feet in a few species in section *Cyrtochila*. Roots of most oncidiums are fine and numerous. Most species are epiphytic, growing in trees, although a few grow on rocks and some are content to grow on the ground among the leaf litter.

Temperature and Humidity Oncidiums grow in many different habitats. They are found from hot, humid tropical lowlands to the cool and misty mountains to some places with almost desert-like climates for much of the year. While oncidiums are more accommodating in their temperature requirements than many orchids, the various species will do best if grown for most of the year in temperatures approximating those in their native habitats. The majority of species grow well in the intermediate temperatures (70 to 85 F days, 60 F nights) suitable for cattleyas. Position those from lowland habitats in the warmer microclimates of the growing area. Those from somewhat higher elevations should be in the cooler areas. The genus has not evolved primarily in high, cool montane areas, as has the closely related genus *Odontoglossum*, and only a few sections, notably *Cyrtochila* and *Cucullata*, are decidedly cool growers. Many species that do reasonably well in intermediate temperatures will grow and flower as well or somewhat better in 50 to 55 F night temperatures. Most oncidiums do not need a seasonal change in temperature to initiate inflorescences.

While there is some variation in humidity needs, for most species the optimum is 50- to 60-percent relative humidity.

Light The majority of oncidiums thrive in the same light conditions as cattleyas, roughly 1,500 to 2,000 foot-candles. Some, such as the terete-leaved species and

RICHARD E. FLEIG

Oncidium Golden Viper 'Vampire', HCC/AOS (*viperinum* x *varicosum*). Grower: Golden Gate Orchids.

the mule-ear group, can tolerate even higher illumination with positive results, while the cool-growing species are best grown with somewhat less light in order to keep the plants cooler. The leaves should be a medium green to slightly yellow- or red-tinged, never dark, glossy green. The leaves of mule-ear species and the dwarf equitant or variegata oncidiums will show evenly distributed tiny dark dots, often on a reddish background, when grown in suitable light. Finally, strong light (short of damaging the foliage), coupled with adequate fertilizer and good roots, will result in robust inflorescences. This can be obtained in a bright greenhouse, a window with a good deal of sun (particularly in winter), or close to the lights in an artificial light setup.

Air Movement As for all orchids, movement of air is requisite. The air should be moist to prevent desiccation, and the flow should be gentle. While sizable fans are normally used in greenhouses, small muffin-type fans obtainable at electronics stores are useful for growing areas in the home. They are small, quiet and use little electricity. Good air circulation tends to result in rapid drying of potting media, something that is essential for healthy roots.

Watering The watering schedule for oncidiums is similar to that for cattleyas, although some species require slightly more frequent watering in order to keep at least the most recent pseudobulb from shriveling. The sections of the genus *Oncidium* differ somewhat in their need for water.

Some enter a substantial rest period of up to several months during which the plant is neither growing nor flowering. Others have a short rest period. A few have none at all because they initiate inflorescences immediately after completing vegetative growth and begin growth anew right after flowering. Those that rest should have somewhat less water during quiescence — but not so little that the pseudobulbs shrivel severely. Hobbyists learn through trial and error how often to water under their particular conditions so that only the older pseudobulbs are slightly shriveled.

Cultivated Sections of the Genus Oncidium

THE FOLLOWING are some sections of the genus *Oncidium* that are popular with hobbyists, listing representative species and indicating special cultural requirements:

Cebolletae (*Onc. cebolleta, Onc. stipitatum, Onc. stacyi, Onc. jonesianum*) — This is the terete-leaved or "rat-tail" group. Grow them very bright, warm and dry. They do best on plaques. The showy flowers are combinations of yellow, brown and white.

Cucullata (*Onc. phalaenopsis, Onc. olivaceum, Onc. nubigenum*) — This is one of the few high-elevation sections in cultivation. They require a cool, humid environment, as for odontoglossums. This is essential. They also require less light than most oncidiums. The small plants produce lovely purple and white flowers.

Crispa (*Onc. crispum, Onc. gardneri, Onc. forbesii, Onc. marshallianum*) — This is a very handsome, large-flowered Brazilian group. The flowers have wing-like petals. Rich brown colors predominate. Grow these on the coolish side of the intermediate range. They do particularly well on plaques under *Cattleya* light conditions.

Cyrtochila (*Onc. macranthum, Onc. lamelligerum, Onc. superbiens*) — These are the giants of the genus, with huge, rambling inflorescences of eye-catching large flowers with small lips. Plants of this group prefer cool temperatures and moderate light.

Glanduligera (*Onc. papilio, Onc. kramerianum, Onc. sanderae*) — These are the butterfly oncidiums, producing one spectacular flower after another at the top of a long inflorescence. The flowers are in shades of red-brown and yellow. The plants prefer *Cattleya* conditions for temperature, light and moisture requirements. They have recently been segregated to the genus *Psychopsis*.

Planifolia (*Onc. sphacelatum, Onc. baueri, Onc. floridanum*) — These are large plants with heavily flowered inflorescences of small yellow-and-brown flowers. These are easy to grow under *Cattleya* conditions or even warmer.

Plurituberculata (*Onc. luridum, Onc. lanceanum, Onc. bicallosum, Onc. splendidum*) — These are the "mule's ear" species, with large, heavy leaves and vestigial pseudobulbs. Plants bear numerous small-to-large flowers in yellow, brown, lavender and white. These species need dry, bright, intermediate to warm conditions.

Rostrata (*Onc. ornithorhynchum, Onc. cheirophorum*) — These dwarf plants produce intensely fragrant flowers in yellows and lavenders. They require *Cattleya* conditions or slightly cooler.

Stellata (*Onc. maculatum, Onc. oliganthum*) — These plants produce star-shaped flowers in large numbers. Their waxy sepals and petals are mottled with chocolate-brown while the lips are white or yellow. These species prefer strong light and temperatures on the cool side of intermediate. Species in section **Oblongata** (*Onc. leucochilum, Onc. tigrinum*) should receive similar treatment.

Synsepala (*Onc. varicosum, Onc. viperinum, Onc. spilopterum, Onc. flexuosum*) — These showy dancing-lady flowers produce enormous yellow lips. Perfect drainage, intermediate-to-cool temperatures and bright light are required to grow these species successfully.

Fertilizing The fertilizer requirements of oncidiums are similar to those for most other epiphytic orchids, such as odonto-glossums.

Potting Oncidiums initiate new roots, often in large numbers, during active vegetative growth. This dictates that the proper time to repot is just after new growth begins but before tender developing root tips can be broken.

Do not disturb a resting or flowering plant because it often will fail to re-establish itself. Most (but not all) oncidiums start new growths between March and May. However, treat each plant in accordance with its cycle. Oncidiums grow well in most standard epiphytic orchid potting media. However, it is essential that drainage be perfect. The roots are quite fine and die if the medium becomes soggy. It also must be fresh. Oncidiums grown in pots normally should be repotted every second year.

A solution used by many to avoid the chore of frequent repotting and the attendant trauma to the plants is to mount rather than pot oncidiums. Tree-fern or cork plaques are the most commonly used, but sections of small limbs from rough-barked trees are particularly useful, and they are aesthetic as well. Each of these mounting media affords excellent drainage except for some tree fern that may be too dense. The only disadvantage is that mounted plants require more frequent watering than those in pots. Oncidiums root strongly on plaques or logs, and with the roots being exposed to air, the plants often do not require remounting for five years or more.

(H. Phillips Jesup is an accredited judge of the American Orchid Society.)

ARTHUR W. HOLST

© CHARLES MARDEN FITCH

Hobbyists in subtropical and tropical climates can grow oncidiums directly on trees where they receive dappled light. Here, *Oncidium varicosum* var. *rogersii* flowers in the garden of Aniel Larnier in Rio Claro, Brazil (above right). A lacy spray from *Oncidium* Taka 'H & R' (Goldiana x *varicosum*) reveals the reason why some growers call oncidiums dancing-lady orchids (right). Grower: Charles Marden Fitch.

Paphiopedilum

By Jack Tonkin

MORE THAN 60 SPECIES OF *PAPH-iopedilum* (paf-ee-oh-PED-i-lum) are found in nature from the high hills of northern India to the lowlands of the Philippines. Magnificent orchids, the paphiopedilums have long been a major part of most collections. A fascinating array of colors and forms and their ease of culture have attracted lifelong admirers.

The relatively recent discovery of several striking species in China, such as the butter-yellow *Paphiopedilum armeniacum*, has sparked unusual excitement among orchid collectors.

All paphiopedilums are characterized by a cuplike lip, called the pouch, and by a prominent dorsal sepal. They are often called slipper orchids, which refers to the shape of the pouch. The plants are primarily terrestrial, although some, like *Paphiopedilum lowii*, may be found growing epiphytically (on trees) or lithophytically (on rocks). They are dwarf to moderate in size, with leaves that are stiff, waxy, or leathery and range from glossy green to superbly mottled. The leaves usually form a fan-shaped tuft. From the center of each new growth an erect scape arises bearing one or more flowers. A few *Paphiopedilum* species — *glaucophyllum*, *stonei* and *rothschildianum* — may produce up to six flowers simultaneously. Mostly the flowers are 2 to 5 inches across in an incredible variety and mixture of colors, lasting perfectly on the plant for six weeks or more. While their blooming season is primarily from mid-autumn through spring, this rule is not absolute. Many modern hybrids flower twice or more each year.

Paphiopedilums are divided into two cultural groups: the warm-growing, mottled-leaved types, like the famous *Paphiopedilum* Maudiae (ideal for beginners), and the cool-growing, green-leaved types. Ideally, the mottled-leaved paphiopedilums need *Cattleya*-like temperatures, while the green-leaved paphiopedilums grow very well in the company of cymbidiums. All paphiopedilums require reasonably cool nights, particularly in the

JOHN J. NELSON

spring when they are setting their buds for the autumn flowering season. Although this requirement makes them difficult to grow in warm areas, their low light requirement does make it possible to keep them cool through shading. Hence both the mottled-leaved and the green-leaved paphiopedilums may be grown almost side by side, although not to the same perfection as they would be were they in growing areas with environments tailored to their specific needs.

Temperature and Humidity The green-leaved types ideally require a minimum night temperature around 50 to 55 F, while the mottled-leaved types need 60 to 65 F at night. Day temperatures should range between 70 F and 80 F, although short periods of moderately higher or lower temperatures will not injure the plants. The humidity should be moderate, between 40 and 50 percent during the day.

Light Paphiopedilums enjoy medium light intensity, requiring 800 to 1,000 footcandles throughout the year for optimum growth. Avoid direct sun, except in the early morning. In the home, move plants

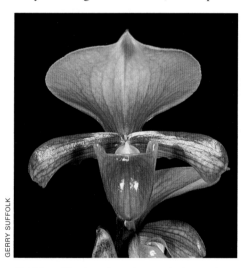

Paphiopedilum tempts novices and advanced growers alike with unusual shapes and colors. Paphiopedilum lowii 'Jennifer', HCC/AOS, (opposite) was grown by Dr. Robert J. Griesbach. Paphiopedilum charlesworthii 'Gladys D', FCC/AOS, (above) was grown by Gladys Darroch.

GERRY SUFFOLK

back from the window at the height of the noonday sun or, ideally, grow them behind a sheer curtain.

Air Movement Moist, vigorous air movement, at a temperature favorable to the plants, is highly recommended to keep the leaves cool and to dry drops of water on the plants, thereby reducing chances of disease. Hot or cold drafts cause buds to blast (brown and die). Consider the position of the plants, especially those on a windowsill.

Watering Although paphiopedilums are sympodial orchids, they do not possess pseudobulbs and hence, like phalaenopsis, must have a regular and constant water supply. This will entail keeping the medium moist but not wet, a technique with which beginners will have to experiment in order to perfect. Water early in the day so that the foliage will dry before temperatures drop at nightfall.

Paphiopedilums typically need watering every five to seven days, but individual conditions require some variance. The potting mix, the humidity surrounding the plants and weather conditions all affect the rate at which plants dry and thus require water.

For those growers using bark as a potting medium, it is extremely important not to permit the plant to dry completely because the bark is then difficult to rewet. Water will channel through the dry mix leaving most of the pot dry. When this happens, submerge the whole pot and mix in a pan of water until moisture has been restored to the pot.

Fertilizing Feed plants in fir bark with a high-nitrogen fertilizer (30-10-20 or 30-10-10 ratio) at half of the recommended strength. Fertilize greenhouse-grown plants three times and then apply plain water for the fourth watering to leach out any salts that have accumulated. For home or windowsill growing, alternate fertilizer and plain water. Plants grown in some of the more complicated mixes consisting of rock, peat, oak leaf mold, etc., should receive fertilizer at a more reduced strength because some of these elements may provide

© CHARLES MARDEN FITCH

ADRIAN R. TEAF

nutrients or may be soured by a high-nitrogen fertilizer at full strength.

Potting Because most paphiopedilums are terrestrial, a medium that drains well but retains moisture is necessary. Straight fir bark is excellent. Finely chopped fir bark ($^1/_8$ inch to $^1/_4$ inch) is preferable to the medium or large chunks used for cattleyas and phalaenopsis. Wet the bark thoroughly before potting any type of orchid in it.

Paphiopedilums grow easily into specimen plants because, with good culture, they branch freely and regularly. Since paphiopedilums are capable of producing flowers on rootless growths, particular care in watering must be taken in growing a specimen plant in order to provide the lovely display of blooms with a healthy, extended root system.

Repot paphiopedilums when the medium has decomposed, the plant has outgrown its pot or when it is appropriate to divide the plant. Although many paphiopedilums will live when divided into single growths with roots, it is preferable to make divisions of no fewer than three growths. Repot and divide immediately following flowering.

In the 1980s, colorful paphiopedilums introduced from China stirred interest in this genus of terrestrial orchids. Two of these species have become extremely popular and are now frequently seen at orchid shows where they often garner awards. *Paphiopedilum armeniacum* 'Jessie', AM/AOS (above left), offers a new dimension in color. Grower: W. Smiles. *Paphiopedilum micranthum* 'Mountain Magic', FCC/AOS (above), produces 5-inch flowers on compact-growing specimens. Grower: Roanoke Orchids.

The procedures for repotting entail clipping off dead roots, positioning the plant in the new container and filling in and around the roots with the compost medium until it reaches just slightly over the base of the plant. Do not bury the plant growths because this encourages rot. The base of each growth should be touching the potting medium to encourage new roots to grow into the medium. Keep watering to a minimum until evidence of new growth is apparent.

Place recently potted paphiopedilums in a shaded area, then move gradually into proper light conditions once new growth begins.

(The late Jack Tonkin was a certified judge of the American Orchid Society.)

Paphiopedilum Relatives

PAPHIOPEDILUM IS part of the Cypripedioideae Alliance, which includes four other genera: *Phragmipedium*, *Selenipedium*, *Cypripedium* and *Mexipedium*, a monotypic genus native to Mexico, where the lone species, *M. xerophyticum*, resides. Few in number of species, these slipper orchids are seen more often in collections where their habit of multiple blooms, combined with unique colors and shapes, affords a striking contrast to their single- and multiple-flowered cousins.

Cypripedium   Among the 50 species of *Cypripedium* (sip-re-PEE-dee-um), which are native to northern temperate areas, are the North American species which are welcome additions to any outdoor garden, provided that they may be induced to establish themselves. They are relatively impossible subjects for greenhouse culture, unless they can be placed in freezing temperatures during the winter months and brought to bloom in the greenhouse at the onset of spring. *Cypripedium calceolus*, the yellow lady's-slipper, is perhaps the best subject for garden culture, blooming freely and establishing itself in large colonies. Purchase seed-grown transplants to prevent disturbing natural populations. Under some circumstances, it is illegal to collect cypripediums from the wild.

Moisture and diffused light are recommended for *Phragmipedium besseae* 'Barbara', AM/AOS. Grower: Barbara Tisherman.

Phragmipedium   More than 20 species of *Phragmipedium* (frag-mi-PEE-di-um) occur from southern Mexico south through Brazil and Peru. *Phragmipedium caudatum*, found from Mexico to Ecuador and Peru, produces leathery, yellow-green leaves up to 2 feet in length and $1^1/2$ to 2 inches wide. The flower stalks rise nearly 2 to 3 feet in the air bearing up to six flowers, uniquely colored in tones of green, brown and crimson, with ribbon-like petals often growing to a length of 3 feet. The red-flowered *Phragmipedium besseae*, from Colombia through Peru, has renewed interest in developing hybrids.

Selenipedium   Giants of the orchid world, a handful of *Selenipedium* (se-lee-ni-PEE-dee-um) species occurs from Costa Rica south through Ecuador and Brazil. Selenipediums are almost too large but for the tallest of greenhouses. They are more at home as specimen plants in tropical gardens. *Selenipedium chica*, a native of Panama, is a tall, reed-like plant. Yellow flowers, with distinctive pouches, top this 15-foot-tall orchid.

PHILIP E. KEENAN

Cypripedium reginae is one of North America's most beautiful native orchids.

Phalaenopsis

By George Vazquez

MOTH ORCHIDS, OR *PHALAENOPSIS* (fail-eh-NOP-sis), are some of the most rewarding orchids for the beginner. Their cultural needs are easily met, with or without a greenhouse. Large mature plants can bloom for three months at a time and, in some cases, bloom twice a year.

Phalaenopsis species range from Asia to the Philippines to New Guinea and parts of Australia. Here the weather is constantly warm and generally provides a humid environment. Among the approximately 50 species are epiphytes (growing on trees) and lithophytes (growing on rocks).

Taxonomists divide the genus into several sections, but the two important sections are *Euphalaenopsis* and *Stauroglottis*. Members of *Euphalaenopsis* have long, arching inflorescences, petals much broader than the sepals and are roundish in outline (*Phalaenopsis amabilis*, *Phalaenopsis*

schilleriana). They usually flower in winter and spring. Section *Stauroglottis* is composed of species that bloom primarily in the summer. The sepals are usually as broad as the petals, and the flowers are smaller and somewhat star-shaped (*Phalaenopsis violacea*, *Phalaenopsis amboinensis*).

Hybridizers are creating new colors in all categories, including the standard-sized phalaenopsis and the miniature multifloras, the latter being characterized by masses of smaller flowers on branching inflorescences. Meeting these goals satisfies the needs of greenhouse growers, who cultivate larger plants, and the windowsill orchidist, who prefers the smaller types.

Phalaenopsis lack pseudobulbs (such as cattleyas and encyclias have) which store water and aid the plants during natural water shortages. They are monopodial and store water only in the leaves. Phalaenopsis receive a great deal of air movement and moisture in their natural habitats and respond favorably when these conditions are duplicated in cultivation.

How to Buy Phalaenopsis

PHALAENOPSIS PLANTS are available in all sizes. Hobbyists can choose to buy flowering specimens — in pot and in spike — or, for a lesser price, one can purchase unflowered seedlings either potted individually or in community pots (left, at bottom), bareroot or still in flask. Out of flask, phalaenopsis are generally sold by leafspan, a measurement from leaf-tip to opposing leaf-tip which accurately indicates the size of the plant for sale.

Though some of the more miniature phalaenopsis may be capable of flowering when they have leafspans as small as 4 inches, most plants are not designated as flowering size until they have an 8-inch-or-more leafspan. Fortunately, phalaenopsis seedlings have a well-deserved reputation for being fast growing, and can flower within a few years once seedlings are removed from the flask in which the seeds were sown. — *Stephen R. Batchelor*

STEPHEN R. BATCHELOR

Temperature and Humidity Although phalaenopsis will grow at temperatures between 60 and 90 F, the optimum maximum is 68 F at night and 85 F during the day. However, plants perform reasonably well at temperatures of 64 F during the night and at warmer day temperatures.

Commercial growers realize that bottom heat is the best source of heat for plants; it warms the pots so the plants grow faster. In the greenhouse, lay inexpensive propagating mats on the benches. These heat the pots and, therefore, warm the plants to a proper temperature, without wasting energy heating the air.

Relative humidity should be 70 percent during the day and 50 percent at night. When night temperatures drop, the relative humidity increases. The easiest way to provide adequate humidity in a home is to fill a plastic or glass tray with gravel or small rocks, and maintain a layer of water in the bottom of the tray. Place the container on the gravel or stones; make sure the bottom of the pot does not touch the liquid. Water evaporating from the tray will bathe the orchid in humidity. Choose a tray approximately the diameter of the orchid's leaf spread to concentrate humidity around the plant.

Air Movement Reliable air movement prevents fungi and bacteria from settling on plants, and will also eliminate spotting of the flowers due to high humidity. Constant cross ventilation is sufficient. However, if a home or apartment must be closed — especially when one is departing for a day or two in warm weather — operate a fan constantly. In a greenhouse, it is important to have air movement 24 hours a day, because relative humidity increases as the night temperature drops and because of the area and size to be ventilated.

Light Provide phalaenopsis with approximately 1,000 foot-candles of light for superior growth. Never allow direct sunlight to reach these orchids. Smaller seedlings require more exact light conditions; strive to maintain the 1,000 foot-candle mark for them. Older and more mature

JOHN D. STUBBINGS

Graceful *Phalaenopsis* Country Charm 'Polly', HCC/AOS (Okauchee x Prairie Du Sac), like many other phalaenopsis hybrids, will flower for several months.

plants are stronger and more tolerant of varying light intensities. Phalaenopsis can bloom and grow when exposed to light intensities ranging from as low as 800 to as high as 1,800 foot-candles. However, they do not continue to grow optimally when

they are stressed, receive inadequate light or their other cultural needs are not met.

An eastern exposure is ideal for phalaenopsis on the windowsill. It is important that the plants are exposed to filtered light, but never direct sunlight. In winter, phalaenopsis need 12 hours of light, and in summer, 14 hours of light. If this is unavailable in the home or apartment, supplement the light source with artificial lights. Morning or afternoon light alone is inadequate for proper growth.

Watering Typical phalaenopsis grown in a pot under an average day temperature of 80 F will dry out about every five to seven days, depending on whether the vessel is clay or plastic and the type of medium used. It is important to understand that the roots of phalaenopsis adhere to the potting medium, and the plant absorbs its water directly from the bark. Thoroughly drench the medium once a week. If the weather is extremely overcast, the medium may not dry out in that time. During the intense heat of summer, the plants can dry out a day or so earlier. Many phalaenopsis growers maintain that the roots should be kept evenly moist, with only a slight drying out time. Small seedlings in 3- and 4-inch pots dry faster, and, therefore, should be watered at shorter intervals. Adjust the watering schedule accordingly.

Water in the morning on a sunny day to allow any water that collects in the crown of the leaves to evaporate. Many beginners kill plants because too much water is left in the crown overnight; this causes crown rot. When it is absolutely necessary to water on an overcast day, be sure to examine the plants

Contemporary hybridizers are reaching beyond the classic white and pink phalaenopsis to develop a new spectrum of eye-catching colors. *Phalaenopsis* Golden Daybreak 'Sunshine Markie' (Wappaoola x Hausermann's Goldcup) (top left), is indicative of breeding traditional novelty yellow phalaenopsis. The intense color of *Phalaenopsis* Golden Buddha 'Raspberry Delight', AM/AOS (Cher Ann x Spica) (middle left), commands attention. Equally beautiful is *Phalaenopsis* Liberty Hill 'Maria Teresa' (Malibu Imp x Fire-water) (left).

CHARLES T. ROWDEN

A different look is offered by *Phalaenopsis* Micro Nova 'von Weltz', AM/AOS (*maculata x parishii*). Grower: S. Robert Weltz Jr.

later and remove any excess water. Either tilt the plant to remove excess water or absorb the fluid with a piece of cloth or tissue.

Fertilizing Give a dilute balanced fertilizer (20-20-20 or 18-18-18) to seedlings. Once the plant has bloomed, it should receive a high-nitrogen fertilizer (30-10-10) twice a month, or, approximately, at every other watering. Avoid applying high-nitrogen fertilizers to small, unflowered seedlings. Although the application of the extra nitrogen promotes faster growth, the plant will not be any stronger and it will bloom accordingly. Fertilizing at every other watering should eliminate a buildup

of minerals because the regular application of plain water every other week flushes out any accumulation of fertilizer salts.

Potting Good drainage is essential regardless of the environment, medium and whether the plants are raised in containers or on plaques. The majority of the phalaenopsis grown in the United States by commercial houses are rooted in fir bark. Generally, small seedlings require a finer bark ($^1/_8$ to $^1/_4$ inch) and larger mature plants a medium grade ($^1/_2$ to $^5/_8$ inch).

Repot phalaenopsis when the plants' foliage is dry; the medium should be moist. To the bark, add a small percentage of coarse sifted peat and equal amounts of perlite (or sponge rock) and charcoal. The additives should be the same size as the bark.

Phalaenopsis potted in medium-size bark mixtures need to be repotted at 14- to 18-month intervals because the bark eventually decomposes. By then, the plant will have outgrown the pot. The better quality fir bark (clean bark without any wood in it) can last two years, and the plant will actually outgrow the pot before the bark breaks down.

(George Vazquez is vice president of Zuma Canyon Orchids in Malibu, California.)

Doritaenopsis Hybrids

DORITAENOPSIS HYBRIDS claim both *Phalaenopsis* and *Doritis* in their ancestry. Those hybrids with a significant amount of *Doritis* in them have characteristic triangular floral shapes, whereas some of the more recent hybrids have so much *Phalaenopsis* in their background that they are indistinguishable from standard *Phalaenopsis* hybrids. Generally, *Doritaenopsis* are noted for their rich, rose-magenta colors. They can be grown like standard phalaenopsis hybrids, although they will tolerate greater light levels. — *Gary Baker*

Vanda

By Robert F. Fuchs

THE MOST POPULAR VANDACEOUS orchids fall into three genera: *Vanda* (VAN-da), *Ascocentrum* (ass-koh-SEN-trum), and *Ascocenda* (ass-koh-SEN-da), an intergeneric hybrid genus between *Vanda* and *Ascocentrum. Euanthe sanderiana*, the species from which most of our common vandaceous hybrids originated, was originally classified as a *Vanda*. It has similar cultural requirements.

All vandaceous orchids are monopodial: growth is from the tip, or crown, of the plant. Lateral buds are present on the main stem, and these may develop into plantlets (keikis) when the plant has attained sufficient size and strength to support them. In accordance with the growth habit of the main stem, each keiki will also continue to grow indefinitely from its tip.

The bloom spikes of vandaceous orchids are produced from the axils of the leaves, which are arranged in two rows. Blooms, which vary in size up to 6 inches, appear in a vast spectrum of colors, and may be clear or marked with checkered or mosaic patterns (tessellations) or spots. The frequent flowering habit of vandaceous hybrids makes them desirable.

Based on their leaf shape, vandaceous orchids can be classified into three groups which have different cultural needs:

• Strap-leaved plants have flat, leathery leaves. This category includes several *Vanda* species — *coerulea, dearei, luzonica, merrillii, tricolor* and *sanderiana* (syn. *Euanthe sanderiana*) — as well as ascocentrums.

• Terete vandas have tapering, pencil-shaped leaves which are circular in cross section. The most common species in this group are *Vanda teres* and *Vanda hookeriana*.

• Semi-teretes are hybrid combinations with some terete species in their background. Their leaves are somewhat pencil-shaped and tapered but not always completely round in cross section.

Temperature and Humidity Vandaceous orchids thrive when the temperature during the day is 65 F or higher and night temperatures are not lower than 55 F. Warm temperatures and bright light promote active growth year-round. These orchids tolerate long periods of hot weather and short periods of cold. Some vandaceous plants can withstand temperatures as low as 38 F for two to three hours, suffering damage to root tips and flower buds, but not the plant itself. Humidity around 80 percent is appropriate on hot sunny days.

Light Vandaceous orchids require strong light. Provide full morning sun when possible. Semi-terete and terete types can be grown in full sun all day in tropical areas where the humidity is high. Strap-leaved plants need additional protection during the hottest part of the day.

Air Movement In the greenhouse, under summer sun, vigorous air movement from a fan is important to keep leaf temperature down and avoid cell damage from heat. For more open conditions — outdoors, in shade houses or lath houses — the natural breeze will balance light, temperature and moisture for healthy growth and flowering. It is important to restrict air movement under colder temperatures.

Watering A high daytime humidity is essential, especially on sunny days, and vandaceous plants outdoors may need watering and misting several times daily during the growing season when the sun is bright. Somewhat less watering is required indoors, although on sunny days plants should be misted once or twice. Limit watering during cooler weather, on cloudy days or after repotting.

Fertilizing Vandaceous orchids require copious quantities of nutrients. Give plants in the greenhouse a solution of a complete fertilizer, such as 20-20-20, weekly during the growing season. Outdoor plants require a heavier concentration of the same fertilizer. During winter, when

R. F. ORCHIDS

growth is slower, apply the same proportions every two weeks rather than weekly. In addition, substitute a fertilizer high in phosphorus (10-30-20) at every third feeding. Further, vitamin and hormone solutions may be added to the fertilizer once a month. To remove built-up salts, flush plants with plain water once a month. Whatever feeding plan is followed, it is important to be faithful to the regimen established.

Potting The best months for potting or repotting vandaceous plants are April and May. Vandaceous plants grow well in any porous medium. Tree fern chunks, coarse bark and charcoal are good choices. Wooden baskets are preferred, but pots can be used if drainage is provided. Suspend plants so that the roots hang freely. Outdoors, grow vandaceous plants in large clay pots or in beds filled with lava rock, tree fern chunks or charcoal. Maintain recently potted specimens under slightly more shaded conditions until they are established.

Because vandaceous plants have large aerial roots, they do not like to be disturbed by removal from their container. Plants

There are two basic leaf shapes in the Old World genus *Vanda: Vanda* Nancy Rodillas 'Best of Show', HCC/AOS (Mabelmae Kamahele x Jennie Hashimoto) (above left), is typical of strap-leaved vandas. Grower: Charles Rodillas. A terete-leaved vanda (above) has pencil-like stems and leaves.

may be moved from smaller to larger baskets. Soak the roots briefly in water until they become pliable, then coil roots around the existing smaller basket and place it in the larger basket. Add a few large pieces of charcoal to hold the smaller basket securely within the larger one. This method minimizes shock to the plant and permits continued, uninterrupted growth.

There are occasions, however, when disturbing the roots cannot be avoided; for example, a rotten basket, or repotting of plants grown in pots. Soak in water, remove as carefully as possible, and place in a solution of vitamins/hormones and fungicide, and allow to soak five minutes. Then pot in a new basket.

(Robert F. Fuchs is owner of R. F. Orchids in Homestead, Florida.)

Vanda Relatives

By Robert F. Fuchs

THE *VANDA* Alliance is known for its durable plants that put forth sprays of lovely flowers. Many are ideal for the tropical and subtropical garden, where they thrive when planted in containers or attached to trees. These orchids respond favorably to the health-care plan prescribed for vandas on the preceding pages.

Aerides Sixty-five species of *Aerides* (AIR-i-deez) hail from tropical Asia. The common name, foxtail orchid, refers to the pendulous inflorescences clothed with waxy, fragrant blooms. Colors vary in shades and combinations of white, apple green and magenta. Aerides produce heavy root structures and do not like to be transplanted. They are, therefore, ideal for cultivating in slat baskets, but may also be grown in pots using coarse, chunky media that permit aeration around the roots.

Arachnis Commonly called the scorpion orchid, *Arachnis* (a-RACK-niss) species are native to areas from the Himalayas to Malaysia. These orchids are popular in the tropics and rapidly climb on trees in warm climates. Flowers are large and showy, with spider-like forms, and spotted or blotched markings. Colors include browns, greens, yellows and lavenders. Arachnis are heavy feeders and require warm, moist conditions. Grow in containers with stakes to support the plants or, outdoors, in beds with support rods.

Ascocentrum *Ascocentrum* (ass-koh-SEN-trum), a Southeast Asian genus of miniature orchids, has three major species — *garayi* (often sold as *Asctm. miniatum*), *curvifolium* and *ampullaceum*. Colors are clear orange, red and fuchsia. Cultural requirements are identical to those of vandas.

RICHARD CLARK

Aerides lawrenciae 'Tru-ford', AM/AOS, enhances the late spring and early summer flowering season with its sprays of waxy flowers. Growers: Trudy and Fordyce Marsh.

© CHARLES MARDEN FITCH

Growers with limited space might want to invest in the miniature *Ascocentrum ampullaceum*. Shown here is the cultivar 'Roman Holiday', AM/AOS. Grower: Joseph Romans.

Renanthera China, Southeast Asia and New Guinea are home to *Renanthera* (ren-ANN-ther-a) species. This genus of beautiful ornamentals includes about 13 species whose blooms range in color from scarlet red through orange to yellowish orange, and are frequently spotted with red. Most renantheras produce glorious, branched inflorescences which provide a dramatic display in greenhouse or garden. These sun-loving plants need high light intensity and frequent fertilizing. They are ideal for outdoor culture in tropical regions, but may not tolerate cold temperatures. Renantheras do well in pots or in beds with large, chunky media which provide good aeration.

Rhynchostylis A fragrant genus from southeastern Asia, *Rhynchostylis* (rink-oh-STYE-liss) produce densely multiflowered inflorescences, similar in appearance to a foxtail, in combinations of white, rose, blue and wine. Of the group, *Rhy. coelestis* is the only one which produces an erect inflorescence; the others are arching to pendulous. Like other fleshy-rooted monopodial orchids, they do not like to be repotted. Basket culture is recommended and frequent fertilizing is required.

Fragrance is a trademark of the densely multiflowered inflorescences of *Rhynchostylis,* including *Rhynchostylis gigantea* var. *alba* 'Cathryn Godden', AM/AOS. Grower: Stephen R. Skoien/Rolfe Horticulture.

YAM TIM WING

Warm and moist conditions are necessary to successfully cultivate *Arachnis hookeriana,* and other *Arachnis,* which are native to the Old World Tropics.

Encyclopedia of Less Common Orchids

By Gary Baker

MARK RISTAU

DON PRUDEN

Anguloas are easily grown and flowered, including *Anguloa ruckeri*, which bears flowers reminiscent of tulips.

A flurry of blooms crowns a well-grown *Brassia verrucosa* 'Great Lakes', CCM/AOS. Grower: Great Lakes Orchids.

Anguloa Ten species of *Anguloa* (an-gyew-LOH-a) are native to Peru, Ecuador, Colombia and Venezuela. Commonly called tulip orchids, in reference to the shape of their flowers, these epiphytes are of easy culture, needing conditions similar to the cool-growing odontoglossums. However, intermediate temperatures are not detrimental. Anguloas require a porous potting mix, bright filtered light, reliable air movement and, when growing, lots of water. The large, rich golden-yellow flowers of *Anguloa clowesii* are among the most impressive of the orchid world. Like other members of this coveted genus, it will tolerate a wide range of environments. Few orchids provide as much delight with as little effort as anguloas.

Brassia Spider orchid is an apt common name for members of the genus *Brassia* (BRASS-ee-a), from Tropical America. They are noted for their unusual, spidery flowers, whose elongated sepals and petals give rise to their common name. Brassias can be grown with cattleyas, although they will appreciate a finer compost than do members of the cattleya group. *Brassia verrucosa*, typical of the genus in that its large flowers are yellowish with dark spots, wants lots of water, light, fertilizer (when actively growing) and warm temperatures. Good air movement is also important.

Bulbophyllum and **Cirrhopetalum** *Bulbophyllum* (bulb-oh-FILL-um) and the closely related *Cirrhopetalum* (see-row-

PET-a-lum) constitute an enormous assemblage of species, native from near sea-level to rather high elevations in mountains in the Old World and New World Tropics. Because of this, prescribing general cultural requirements for the entire genus is difficult; the hobbyist needs to investigate the temperature requirements of any species acquired. Most species in cultivation

More than 5,000 flowers borne on 110 inflorescences covered this *Bulbophyllum medusae* 'Miami', CCM/AOS, which is admired for its bizarre flowers. Grower: Jones & Scully, Inc.

forgive abuse. Provide lots of light, water, air movement and room — many are rampant growers. Flowers may be tiny to quite large. *Bulbophyllum lobbii*'s unusual, 4-inch-wide, fragrant flowers are yellow to buff yellow, spotted with purple.

Temperatures

THE TEMPERATURE requirements of the orchids in this listing of less common genera are referred to as cool, intermediate and warm. The minimum night temperatures for these categories are provided below:

Cool growing: 50 to 55 F
Intermediate: 55 to 65 F
Warm growing: 60 to 65 F minimum
Each of these can increase 10 to 20 F during the day.

Cycnoches *Cycnoches* (SIK-no-keez) are often called swan orchids. These New World orchids, about 12 species in all, produce their captivating flowers (like inverted swans) on large plants which love heat, humidity, fertilizer, light and water when actively growing. However, reduce moisture on completion of the new growths. The large thin leaves are susceptible to infestations of red spider mites; treat them accordingly if seen (a silvery appearance to the underside of the leaves is a common

Heat, humidity and fertilizer are recommended for *Cycnoches chlorochilon* during the growing season, usually in spring and summer.

Disa Foam 'San Francisco', FCC/AOS (Betty's Bay x *uniflora*) is adapted to cooler temperatures. Grower: Pui Y. Chin.

clue). *Cycnoches chlorochilon* (syn. *Cycnoches ventricosum*) produces fragrant, green flowers which resemble a small flock of swans swimming upside down.

Disa *Disa* (DEE-za) *uniflora*, one of the most brilliantly red orchids known, is typical of the cooler-growing members of this terrestrial African genus. It requires moisture, cool temperatures, a shallow container and a potting compost with lots of chopped sphagnum, coarse sand and humus. Protect from bright light, and see that adequate ventilation is given.

Dracula Treat members of *Dracula* (DRA-kew-la) like masdevallias: fine mix, ample shade and moisture, cool temperatures and high humidity. Because many species in this Neotropical genus produce pendent (*Dracula bella*) or semi-pendent (*Dracula vampira, Dracula chimaera*) inflorescences, it is critical that most species be planted in containers which allow these

inflorescences to emerge. Otherwise the flowers will never be seen. Baskets made of some durable mesh work fine; aluminum gutter mesh is widely employed. Baskets constructed of wooden slats work satisfactorily. A few species, such as *Dracula gigas*, do have rather erect inflorescences. Copious water and perfect drainage are essential. Keep fertilizer to a minimum; excess dissolved salts in their water, be it from fertilizer or naturally occurring salts, will cause leaf-tip die-back. New Zealand sphagnum moss has been widely used as a potting medium with considerable success.

Gongora New World gongoras (gon-GOR-ah) need conditions similar to those of *Stanhopea*. However, since their inflorescences arch outward from the plant and are not pendulous, gongoras do not need to be cultivated in slatted baskets. Richly fragrant, these are sometimes called Punch and Judy orchids. The American Tropics is home to 25 species.

Ludisia Few orchids are grown for their foliage. However, *Ludisia discolor* (syn. *Haemaria discolor*) is the best-known member of a select small assemblage of genera known as the jewel orchids. Dark leaves, highlighted with white or yellowish veins, are a trademark of *Ludisia* (loo-DIS-ee-ah), with one species found in Southeast Asia and China. *Ludisia discolor* probably survives under lower light better than any other commonly grown orchid. A terrestrial, it does appreciate a potting mix rich in humus. Never allow it to dry, protect it from bright light and keep it warm. Unlike its more delicate, strikingly beautiful allies, such as *Macodes* (ma-KOH-deez) and *Anoectochilus* (ah-nek-toh-KYE-luss), this species will survive in a home without being kept in a terrarium. If room air does not become too dry, this species can make a magnificent specimen indoors. During late autumn through spring, the plants become covered with spires of white flowers.

Among the many exciting draculas is *Dracula chimaera* 'Joyce', AM/AOS. Grower: Ralph Kratky.

Lycaste *Lycaste* (lye-KASS-tee) species and hybrids may be evergreen or deciduous, and all like water curtailed when new growth is nearly completed. Obviously, the deciduous types resent being watered when they have no leaves. When actively growing, copious water and ample fertilizer are needed. Protect the large thin leaves from strong sunlight, watch for signs of red spider mite damage (silvery appearance to the leaves) and see that good air movement is provided. *Lycaste skinneri* (syn. *Lycaste virginalis*), the national flower of Guatemala, is generally regarded as the most beautiful of the two dozen species native to the New World Tropics. It occurs in both colored (palest pink to richest rose) and white forms. Pot lycastes in a finely textured compost, one that permits good drainage, yet retains moisture. Lycastes do require considerable space.

Gongora horichiana bears its unusual flowers on pendent inflorescences.

Maxillaria *Maxillaria* (max-sil-LAIR-ee-a) is native to a variety of habitats in the New World Tropics. Fortunately, many of the 300 species tolerate a variety of conditions. Some species, such as *Max. tenuifolia* (with its powerful coconut cream-pie fragrance), will likely thrive despite a hobbyist's unintended efforts to kill them. Give maxillarias a finely textured compost

Lycaste Wyldfire 'Chelsea', AM/AOS (Balliae x Wyld Court) flowers in winter or early spring. Grower: S. Robert Weltz Jr.

Expect the scent of coconut from the flowers of *Maxillaria tenuifolia* 'Alisha', HCC/AOS. Grower: Jay Mullen.

that permits rapid drainage, ample moisture (when new growths are being made) and bright light. The smaller-growing species thrive when attached to a piece of tree fern, cork or other support. A few species will need cool temperatures. Determine the temperature requirements of any species acquired.

Neofinetia *Neofinetia falcata* is a choice small-growing species from Japan whose copiously produced white flowers are blessed with an almost-overpowering vanilla-chocolate fragrance. Treat it like a small *Vanda*. *Neofinetia* (nee-o-fin-AY-tee-a) tolerates near-freezing temperatures on occasion.

Pleurothallis *Pleurothallis* (plur-o-THAL-lis) is related to *Stelis, Octomeria, Porroglossum* and other genera which are lumped into a general group called pleurothallids. All of these need a porous potting mix, copious water, much air movement, considerable shade, coolish temperatures and a fine compost because of their very fine, wiry roots. Cultural conditions similar to those suggested for *Masdevallia* will meet the needs of the more than 1,000 Neotropical *Pleurothallis.*

Restrepia Culture for *Restrepia* (res-TREP-ee-ah) is comparable to most masdevallias and other pleurothallids: fine-textured mix, good drainage, shade and protection from dry air and hot temperatures. However, restrepias tolerate warmer temperatures than are generally associated with that group, which makes them easier to grow outside of the New England and the cool Pacific-coast regions. *Restrepia antennifera* and its myriad associated species are typical of the New World genus in bearing many successive flowers with each leaf; the conspicuous, attractive flowers are quite large for the small plants. The leaves, with a portion of the subtending "petiole" (in actuality, a modified stem termed a ramicaul), may be cut from the plant after they have produced a number of flowers, and, when inserted in potting mix, will often produce new plantlets, much as an African violet does.

Stanhopea Stanhopeas (stan-HOPE-ee-a) are easily grown into large, dramatic hanging-basket specimens. Because of the pendent nature of their inflorescences, stanhopeas must be grown in wooden or wire baskets. Line the basket with wire mesh, coconut-husk fiber or New Zealand sphagnum moss so the potting mix will not wash out of the container. A loose compost that drains well is necessary. Copious water, ample fertilizer and good light are needed. Stanhopeas tolerate a wide range of temperatures. Protect the large, broad

Neofinetia falcata is known in its native Japan as *Fuku-rin,* meaning "rich and noble orchid." Grower: Charles Marden Fitch.

Pleurothallis fit on the windowsill and under lights. Try *Pleurothallis truncata* 'J & L', CBM/AOS. Grower: Mr. and Mrs. L. B. Kuhn.

leaves from sunburn. Allow the plants to develop into specimens to get the best floral displays. Among the 25 species native to Tropical America is *Stanhopea tigrina*, with its massive yellow and maroon flowers. It is typical of the genus in that all bear large, bizarre flowers which resemble birds of prey from some extraterrestrial source and which emit a near overpowering fragrance.

Vanilla   Of the approximately 25 species in this genus, the Mexican *Vanilla planifolia* is by far the most commonly seen. *Vanilla* (va-NIL-la) is an unusual genus in that its members are vines which can grow many feet in length. *Vanilla planifolia* is the species from whose fruits (commonly called "beans") the flavoring vanilla is obtained. The clusters of small yellowish flowers resemble those of some unusual *Cattleya*. *Vanilla* is terrestrial and epiphytic, and needs a humus-laden compost through which water drains rapidly.

Restrepia guttulata 'Willow Pond', CBM-CCM/AOS, is of interest to the connoisseur of miniatures. Growers: Ann and H. Phillips Jesup

Try one with peat moss or leaf mold mixed with fine bark or chopped tree fern. Provide some sort of pole to which the aerial roots of the vines can attach. A support for an ivy or philodendron would suffice. Good drainage and ample water, strong light, high humidity and warm temperatures induce healthy growth. Cultivate vanilla with cattleyas. One word of warning: do not expect to harvest your own vanilla beans until after the vines have grown 15 feet or so in length. Then, when it flowers, it is necessary to hand-pollinate the flowers, keeping in mind that there is a flap over the stigmatic surface of the flower. In other words, buy vanilla flavoring from the store and grow *Vanilla* purely as an ornamental.

Zygopetalum Sixteen species of *Zygopetalum* (zye-go-PET-a-lum) are native to South America. These wonderfully fragrant orchids are easy to grow. Because of their large fleshy roots, a medium that is porous and drains easily is essential; try medium- to large-sized bark or pumice. Zygopetalums grow rapidly and large so they need room to expand and space for the 2-foot-tall leaves to develop. They thrive in cool or intermediate temperatures and are successfully grown outdoors in frost-free coastal California. They are copious drinkers and relish abundant fertilizer during periods of active growth in spring and summer. Fragrant *Zygopetalum intermedium* produces tall spikes of sizable green, white and blue-violet flowers.

(The late Gary Baker was an AOS judge and wrote for various AOS publications.)

Grow *Stanhopea frymirei* 'Cal Dodson', CBM/AOS, in a hanging basket to permit display of its pendent inflorescences. Grower: FL Stevenson.

Vanilla beans are the seed capsules of several species of *Vanilla*, including *Vanilla tahitensis*.

Zygopetalum mackayi 'Oso Grande', HCC/AOS. Grower: Orchids of Los Osos.

RESOURCES

Renantheras are sun-loving orchids ideally suited to subtropical and tropical gardens. One magnificent selection is *Renanthera* Memoria Marie Killian 'Eric's Red Imp', AM/AOS (Merritt Island x John Tew). Grower: Dr. Lawrence Schweitzer.

Month-by-Month Checklist

By Robert M. Scully Jr.

JANUARY

■ The *Phalaenopsis* flowering cycle is about to start. Constant air circulation is essential to avoid *Botrytis*-spotted blooms. Water carefully to keep flowers dry and to minimize risks of soft rot in the fleshy leaves. Fertilize sparingly with a liquid or granular formula, and only when the medium is moist. Begin careful monitoring for scale and mealybugs on the inflorescences and undersides of leaves.

■ Tie up *Cattleya* pseudobulbs. Watch for signs of red spider mites on the undersides of leaves or scale in the sheathing on pseudobulbs. Remove the sheathing (cataphylls) carefully so as not to nick the soft tissue of the newest pseudobulbs, which could result in rot or the introduction of virus.

■ Continue to water sparingly, or not at all, those *Dendrobium* species that require a dormant period before flowering this spring (*Den. lindleyi* [syn. *Den. aggregatum*], *Den. chrysotoxum*, *Den. farmeri*, *Den. densiflorum* and *Den. nobile* or its hybrids). As the buds emerge, gradually increase the watering frequency and amount. Do not expose evergreen-type hybrids to temperatures below 60 F, or plants in flower may drop leaves and buds.

■ Fertilize moist *Vanda* baskets or pots at least twice this month if light levels are sufficient. Many of the popular Thai hybrids and the African angraecoids begin their winter flowering now, so watch for signs of inflorescences; "help" them away from the main stem of the plant to ensure proper display. Maintain high humidity in the root zone, particularly for those plants in slatted baskets. Mist the roots daily with a light spray from a spray bottle or hose.

■ Keep the humidity conditions high around cymbidiums to prevent shriveling of the pseudobulbs and to prolong flowering. Later varieties are beginning to push up their inflorescences; watering frequency and volume is important to support their development. Cool temperatures are beneficial.

■ Do not allow the roots of paphiopedilums to dry out. On a windowsill, use a pebble tray, with water in the pebbles, to increase humidity. Keep water out of the sensitive pouches; accumulated moisture shortens flower life. Watch for insects, particularly red spider mites, on the foliage.

© CHARLES MARDEN FITCH

Proper staking produces quality displays in phalaenopsis, including *Phalaenopsis* Cassandra 'Cumulus', HCC/AOS (*equestris* x *stuartiana*). Grower: Paphanatics unLtd.

FEBRUARY

■ Observe plants carefully for signs of disease and insects. Do not overlook companion plants, such as ferns and aroids; they often provide cover for insect populations that may spread to orchids.

■ Attend to humidity needs. Too often, growers fail to provide adequate moisture in the heated atmosphere, and this leads to dehydration of plants and reduced flower life. Avoid having heated or air-conditioned drafts blowing directly on orchids, whether they are in the growing area or in the home or office for display.

■ An occasional fertilizer treatment is appropriate for cattleyas, even though temperature and light conditions are not ideal for growth. Apply dyed fertilizers with care to prevent staining the blooms rising in the sealed sheaths. Sometimes it is necessary to split open a sheath with a sterile blade to reduce pressure on the emerging buds or to allow accumulated condensation (possibly from fluctuating temperatures) to dissipate.

■ Apply a weak fertilizer solution to *Phalaenopsis*. Be careful not to splatter the flowers or they will stain. As with any orchid, do not fertilize a dry pot; water today and fertilize tomorrow. Phalaenopsis exude a honey-like substance on the developing inflorescence; it attracts scale insects. Watch for signs of any problem that could be spot-treated before it becomes a major situation. Avoid spraying insecticides on blossoms.

■ Watch for flower buds on dendrobiums — *Den. lindleyi, Den. nobile* hybrids, *Den. superbum* (syn. *Den. anosmum*), and other deciduous species and hybrids. These have longer-lasting flowering when exposed to cooler night temperatures as the blooms open and mature. Avoid dousing open flowers when watering; give slightly more water to these plants (which have been kept reasonably dry prior to flowering) once they begin to bloom. Continue to protect evergreen-type dendrobiums from low temperatures that may cause leaf loss.

■ Stake *Cymbidium* inflorescences that have emerged from the mass of foliage on these winter-spring bloomers. Maintain temperatures at 50 to 60 F to keep the flowers opening slowly. Dramatically higher temperatures and hot drafts cause bud drop.

■ Do not permit *Miltonia* and *Odontoglossum* to dry out, because this is a critical time for flower-spike developmemt. Stake the spikes. Apply a weak liquid fertilizer just before the flowers begin to appear.

MARCH

■ Sheaths will soon emerge on *Cattleya mossiae* hybrids. Monitor their development so that moisture does not accumulate in the sheath and cause bud blast.

■ *Phalaenopsis* grown in New Zealand sphagnum moss rapidly increase in one season. Make sure that the moss does not deteriorate before the flowering season, because a healthy root system is particularly important for the many flowers a plant may produce. Poor roots and lots of blooms may cause plants to become severely dehydrated, even to the point where reviving them is difficult.

■ Fragrant *Dendrobium anosmum* (syn. *Dendrobium superbum*)and *Dendrobium nobile* hybrids flower this month. Do not neglect watering because dryness can cause bud drop in all dendrobium species and hybrids.

■ Growth may be active in some pleurothallid species. Maintain a regular fertilizer program, perhaps once every two weeks with a quarter- or half-strength solution. Watch for emerging flower spikes; guide them through the leaves.

■ *Cyrtopodium punctatum,* the cow-horn orchid, blooms now. Its yellow flowers are spotted with mahogany brown and look most curious among the leafless, horn-like pseudobulbs.

■ The last of the *Cycnoches chlorochilon* may be blooming this month. Gorgeous chartreuse flowers emit a distinctive sweet fragrance.

■ *Oncidium papilio,* the butterfly orchid, may be pushing out the first in a series of many buds, and subsequently flowers, that will appear through the spring and early summer. It is a perpetual bloomer. Do not sever the inflorescence because it will continue to produce flowers year after year. Even though *Onc. papilio* has rather hard leaves, suggesting that it will tolerate a lot of light (like cattleyas), experience shows that it will grow well and flower even better in bright *Phalaenopsis*-like conditions.

APRIL

■ *Cattleya aclandiae* and *Cattleya forbesii* produce flowers in the first half of the month that usually last for weeks. *Cattleya mossiae* and its hybrids, well-known for their spectacular, long-lasting heads of 6-inch, fragrant blossoms, flower later, sometimes in May. These make excellent cut flowers.

■ Begin repotting this month by shifting and dividing (if necessary) those cattleyas that flowered earlier this year and are beginning to

Community pots of orchid seedlings, like these phalaenopsis, make it possible for growers to obtain many plants at reasonable cost.

New shoots and roots on cattleyas signal it is time to repot. Perform the job before the roots are as long as those shown here to avoid snapping off the brittle green root tips.

the flowers are open or damage may result. Check the undersides of the leaves for scale or developing mite infestations near the midvein. The scale may be treated as suggested above. For mites, however, application of a carefully directed miticide spray may be necessary to halt the increasing population.

■ Maintain a monthly fertilizer schedule for flowering plants. Fertilize more often as new leaves emerge.

MAY

■ Identify orchids that need repotting over the next 60 days; consider tagging them with different colored labels (to indicate anticipated repotting week). Assemble the necessary potting materials.

■ Recycle clay and plastic pots. Make sure they have been thoroughly washed and sterilized. Soak pots in a RD-20/Physan solution (follow label instructions) to kill most pathogens. Before soaking, carefully scrub away algae and salts residues with a stiff brush. Heat sterilize clay pots (350 F in the stove oven for one or two hours) to eliminate virus particles. Sterilizing wire products (stakes and clips) is acceptable. Recycling tree fern and wood baskets and any potting or drainage material (pot shards or polystyrene chips) is not recommended.

■ Before dividing a cattleya, get a head start. With a sterile and very sharp knife, sever the rhizome completely or even partially (at the appropriate point to insure that it will have at least three or four pseudobulbs per division) while the plant is still in its original pot. After new growth emerges (weeks later), complete the repotting project. When securing new divisions in their pots, use some cushioning material, e.g., a redwood chip or an osmunda pad, between the rhizome clip and the rhizome to prevent trauma to the sensitive plant tissue.

■ Feed all cattleyas (except those just repotted) every two weeks. Water more frequently; plants need more water to efficiently utilize increased food and light levels that are typically available now.

■ Repot phalaenopsis that have finished flowering. Wait for the emergence of a new leaf in the crown before proceeding. When you repot, remove the old inflorescence and eliminate all rotten or completely dehydrated roots. Fertilize repotted plants only when new roots become visible; select a fertilizer formula tailored to use on the medium in which the phalaenopsis now grow. Consider a spraying program with a recommended fungicide.

produce new growth. Repot only when the new growth is emerging to take advantage of the plant's tendency to make new roots when it is forming new pseudobulbs. Fertilize twice a month; with longer days and warmer temperatures, the plants can use more food.

■ *Encyclia cordigera* (syn. *Epidendrum atropurpureum*) should be blooming profusely. The spicy fragrance will last for several weeks. *Encyclia cordigera* makes an excellent specimen. Consider shifting this epiphyte to a log cabin-style wood basket when flowering is completed.

■ *Laelia cinnabarina, Laelia flava, Laelia harpophylla* and perhaps *Laelia milleri* will flower this month. When blooming ceases, shift the plants to a larger pot. All of these rupicolous laelias need to have their roots in a cool medium. Consider using clay pots for the evaporative cooling effect that results when they are drying after a thorough watering.

■ Inspect the flower stems of *Phalaenopsis* for scale. Look for signs of a honey-like substance at the nodes and also on the back sides of the flowers; these are favorite haunts for armored and soft scale. If these pests are present, you may spot-treat with an alcohol swab or wipe on a light application of an insecticidal soap; again, it is not advisable to spray when

■ This is probably the ideal month to complete repotting of lady's-slippers. Prepare a terrestrial mix with fresh ingredients. Remove dead roots and keep as many growths together as practical. Monitor light levels to be sure that these plants receive adequate shade and cool temperatures. Keep root-zone moisture levels reasonably high; occasionally mist the foliage.

■ Finish repotting cymbidiums. If the medium is in good condition (maybe a year old), move the plant from one container to another with the addition of a small volume of new medium; avoid disturbing the roots, especially any new root tips. Keep the pots moist and syringe the foliage frequently, particularly if the plant has been moved into brighter light.

■ Some vandas and ascocendas may need more room for root development. Drop those in a log-cabin-style wooden basket into a larger-size basket with the roots either wound around in the space between the two boxes or worked through the slats of the new basket. With longer and warmer days, vandas grow vigorously; fertilize three to four times this month with a liquid or soluble 1:1:1 ratio formula (7-7-7 or 20-20-20).

JUNE

■ Orchids repotted earlier should be showing new roots and growths. Fertilize more often. Apply a concentration of at least two teaspoons per gallon of water (at delivery) of soluble formulations or the equivalent of 250 ppm (parts per million) in liquid formulas. With more light (sun is higher and more intense for more hours each day), higher day and night temperatures, excellent air circulation and a fresh (or at least wholesome) growing medium, the orchids will consume more nutrients. Robust growths will produce more high-quality flowers next season.

■ It was recommended in May that, before dividing cattleyas, a cut be made in the rhizome behind a pseudobulb on which an "eye" could be found. Where a growth has begun to emerge from this eye, remove the division and repot. If there is a growth response on only one-half of the plant, wait a while longer for the other part to respond. Repot when a new growth is about 1 to 2 inches long. Be careful when handling the division to avoid damaging the fragile emerging shoot.

■ Finish repotting cattleyas in June. Cattleyas outside in the subtropics must be protected from excessive rainfall. Apply protective fungicides when the relative humidity levels begin to hover consistently in the 70 percent-plus range.

■ Complete repotting *Phalaenopsis*. Check the turgidity of the foliage and condition of the roots of specimens still in bloom. June's longer-and-warmer days increase the moisture requirements of flowering plants. Do not be greedy. A phalaenopsis will deteriorate rapidly if forced to carry its inflorescence too long in a stressful cultural environment. Repot rather than lose a plant. If in doubt as to whether the potting medium will be good for another year, opt to repot now. Remember to repot phalaenopsis seedlings, too. Those repotted from 2-to 3-inch pots now will have a good chance of blooming next winter. Fertilize at least three or four times this month and for the balance of the summer at the same rate as described for cattleyas above. Protect *Phalaenopsis* from overhead water, both artificial irrigation and rain, and water early in the day so the foliage is dry by nightfall.

■ Repot the last few dendrobiums. Test some of the aggregate media that are available. Growers in temperate zones have experienced positive results with lava rock (like the Hawaiians use). Adding some nutrient-holding fir bark chips to the mix may be beneficial. Consider mounting deciduous cane-type dendrobiums on tree-fern or cork plaques.

■ Vandas need high light intensity for growth, but protect them from direct sun. Make the transition from the protected environs of the winter greenhouse to the harsher outdoor con-

JOSEPH VOLPE

Intense light is necessary to flower vandas, ascocentrums and ascocendas, including *Vanda sanderiana* 'Chester Kawakami', AM/AOS. Grower: Floradise Orchids.

ditions gradually. If moving the specimens higher in the glass house, take the same precautions. Avoid burning by occasionally misting the leaves during the transition period. Continue to fertilize frequently, about three to four times each month.

JULY

■ Repotting should be completed by July. If this task is performed now, provide follow-up care. Increase humidity around the orchid. Place the specimen on a water-filled pebble tray, even in the greenhouse (but water the fresh medium much less frequently). Or, place the entire repotted plant inside a plastic bag perforated with a few holes to provide ventilation and keep the plant out of direct sun. When new roots emerge, remove the bag and initiate regular treatment. This plastic bag incubator is effective year-round when nursing highly stressed plants.

■ Observe roots when repotting. Notice if all of the roots are plump and white, and if some are flattened or dried (appearing to consist of only a stringy central core). Chances are that both kinds will be present. These dried root remnants are the result of a normal aging process. Cut them away when repotting, taking care not to injure the orchid. This is a smart move, because too many decaying roots soon become mush and accelerate the deterioration of the mix.

Despite a paucity of orchid flowers during the summer, a few continue to add interest. Among these is the genus *Doritaenopsis*. Shown here is *Doritaenopsis* Memoria Doctor Ho 'Plantation', AM/AOS (*Phal.* Paifang's Queen x *Dtps.* Happy Valentine). Grower: The Orchid Plantation.

■ Blackened root tips on fleshy roots can mean that the water contains an excessive concentration of soluble salts or that the clay pot surfaces are bonding with or accumulating excess salts, either from normal water supply or your regular fertilizer treatments. Some growers, facing the challenges of dealing with poor water quality, have resorted to using deionized water or, better yet, rainwater. Scrub away the visible salt crusts capping the top edges of clay pots before recycling them. Leach the medium thoroughly once or twice a month.

■ Another root condition to avoid is the development of snow mold, a white fungus that looks just like what the name implies. Snow mold can appear on the surface of the potting medium, but more likely it will develop in the root zone. An insidious problem, the mold often escapes detection until the root mass has been smothered in a rapidly deteriorating medium. The condition is treatable. Affected plants will not be lost. However, snow mold seems to appear most frequently when media are kept too wet, causing the roots to rot and the substrate to become a soggy mess. Snow mold is a saprophytic fungus that actually works to hasten the potting medium's decomposition. Monitor watering practices to avoid the problem. Blend a small amount of redwood chips in the potting material to increase the acidity and deter snow mold. Repot affected plants, and be sure to remove all of the old medium before rinsing the roots in a weak solution of Physan.

■ Maintain the fertilizer regime at the highest frequency. The more growth achieved now, the more flowers the orchids can support in their blooming seasons.

■ Insects are most active during the warm months. Inspect the undersides of leaves for undesirable creatures in hiding. Remove dried sheathing (cataphylls) on cattleya pseudobulbs to eliminate a hiding place.

AUGUST

■ August is likely to be the hottest month. Work diligently to meet the humidity and air-circulation requirements necessary to raise healthy orchids. In the greenhouse, spray water on the floor, bench tops or outer surfaces of clay pots one or more times every day during the most severe periods. Indoors, it may be necessary to move orchids back from the window to prevent intense sunlight from injuring leaves.

■ Summer's higher temperatures, brighter light conditions and longer days induce orchids to manufacture the greatest amount of carbo-

Keikis with roots on dendrobiums can be removed and potted individually to multiply a plant collection.

fans to promote sufficient air circulation. Do not irrigate from above (to avoid splashing unseen disease inoculum from plant to plant). Instead, water plants pot to pot, and do not bang (bruise) the turgid leaves with the hose nozzle. Feed these rapid growers frequently to develop the strongest root systems and largest leaves possible prior to the winter flowering season.

■ Cattleya growers should still be enjoying many of the advanced yellow hybrids from *Cattleya dowiana*. Some of the large-flowered hybrids of *Cattleya bicolor* may open this month. Both groups are showy, long-lasting and fragrant. Avoid splashing water on the blossoms, and place flowering specimens where air circulation is sufficient to reduce the risk of a *Botrytis* infection. Continue to fertilize cattleyas frequently. As new growths mature, tie them up carefully to promote upright development of the pseudobulbs.

■ Summer growing conditions are ideal for hybrids of *Aerides, Ascocentrum, Rhynchostylis* and *Vanda*. Feed aggressively and provide high humidity for optimum responses.

SEPTEMBER

■ Autumn is nearly here, so expect to witness the emergence of buds on many orchids, from the cattleyas and vandas to cycnoches, catasetums and even warm-growing miltonias. Select an ideal spot for the plant. This will likely be atop an inverted pot for those types with arching or pendulous inflorescences, or it may mean moving the plant to the upper level on your step bench. Position the plant so that it receives ideal light for most of the day. Support the inflorescence as it emerges. Sometimes it is necessary to open the sheath to prevent the accumulation of excess moisture around the developing buds, even before they emerge.

■ This is *Dendrobium phalaenopsis* season. Long, arching sprays of flat, dark red-puple to white or pink saucer-like blossoms provide weeks of satisfaction. *Nobile*-type hybrids should continue to be maintained on a nitrogen-free fertilizer program. Water sparingly to keep the pseudobulbs from dehydrating.

■ Autumn is typically the end of the growing season for *Catasetum* and *Cycnoches*. Plants may produce flowers from pseudobulbs with leaves, or in some instances, from bulbs that have already lost their leaves. Watch the undersides of the leaves to control spider mites which seem to find these delicacies just as the foliage reaches its prime or plants are about to

hydrates when provided with adequate fertilizer. Apply a slightly diluted concentration (two teaspoons of soluble fertilizer per gallon of water) once each week.

■ Warm temperatures cause insect populations to increase. Pay attention to pest-control management. Observe your plants carefully and spray for both insects and disease when first noticed. Endure the discomforts of patrolling the hot, muggy atmosphere of a greenhouse now in order to maintain healthy orchids this autumn and next winter.

■ The *nobile*-type dendrobiums are popular. While many are sold in the warmer latitudes, growers there find this epiphytic orchid a little difficult to flower. In order to promote the gradual shift from active growth (spring to early summer) to the flowering cycle, withhold nitrogen. Experienced growers say that accumulated nitrogen from excessive application through the year may be the reason why these orchids are sometimes reluctant to bloom.

■ Current high temperatures are particularly stressful for phalaenopsis. In some areas, humidity conditions are quite high. Excessive heat and humidity promote bacterial *Pseudomonas* infections on the fleshy leaves. Keep light levels subdued and temperatures below 85 F; it may be necessary to operate additional

bloom. Support the basal racemes of catasetums as they emerge; and consider putting the plants on inverted pots to provide room for them to hang freely.

■ Of the three popular pansy orchids — *Miltonia* x *bluntii*, *Miltonia roezlii* and *Miltonia spectabilis* — the latter is probably the most showy. The reddish purple flowers of *Milt. spectabilis* var. *moreliana* usually appear singly and last for weeks. The racemes can be very heavy, even when carrying only a single bloom, so provide support.

■ This is the principal blooming season for *Euanthe sanderiana* (syn. *Vanda sanderiana*), the foundation for large-flowered modern vandaceous hybrids. Position plants so that the inflorescences will grow out of the leaves toward the light; help uncooperative types by placing a thin bamboo stick between the emerging inflorescence and the flattened form of the leaves, thereby forcing the raceme outward.

OCTOBER

■ Plan for winter-like conditions. Decide where you will keep your most sensitive plants when the first cold arrives. Inspect the covering of your growing house to see if it is intact or needs replacing before the winds, which usually accompany a rainy cold front, strip the structure. Determine if the greenhouse is reasonably airtight to minimize heat loss and/or the development of cold water drips (condensation). Test your heaters to ascertain that they are operating correctly. Verify that your fuel tank (gas or oil) is filled, that the vent systems are functional and that all electrical control devices — including your temperature alarm system — are working.

■ Observe the rate at which your plants dry after each watering. With cooler and shorter days, expect a longer term between waterings. Watch those plants that have been in the brightest light through the summer because they are probably going to need some extra watering when first brought in from the outdoors.

■ *Sophronitis coccinea*, *Cattleya luteola*, *Laelia pumila*, *Encyclia cochleata*, *Epidendrum ciliare* and *Epidendrum pseudepidendrum* flower now. These range in size from the diminutive first three to the tall and spectacular last-named species. Flowers range from lavender (*L. pumila*) to green to orange-red and on through the yellow or greenish tones of the others.

■ *Phalaenopsis lueddemanniana* var. *hieroglyphica* (syn. *Phal. hieroglyphica*) flowers in the autumn. Its pale yellow flowers are distinctively marked with well-defined brown lines arranged randomly on the sepals and petals. These long-lasting flowers are fragrant. *Phalaenopsis equestris* and *Phalaenopsis lindenii* may also show their best now; the former may be everblooming through spring. *Phalaenopsis lindenii* will arouse curiosity with its attractively striped lip.

■ The first flowers of *Catasetum pileatum* and its hybrids should be seen now. Handle all catasetums with care when the blooms open. Even a minor jarring of the plant or direct contact with the flower can cause the flowers to eject their pollen-carrying anther caps, resulting in a much shortened flower life.

NOVEMBER

■ Organize plants so that all are exposed to optimum light levels. Be wary of insects. Be vigilant and turn leaves to look for pests. Eradicate them quickly when they are found.

■ From now through spring is a great time to visit orchid nurseries. Growers appreciate visitors touring the facilities without a large purse or bulky camera bag that may whack the plants that overhang the crowded benches along narrow aisles.

■ Re-tie each cattleya to support the newly produced growths. Position cattleyas with the lead (newest growth) facing the direction of the principal light source. New growths of *Cattleya skinneri* may already have some dried sheaths; do not remove them.

■ Observe emerging phalaenopsis inflorescences (casually referred to as spikes) between the lower leaves near the base of the plant. As these spikes push upward, carefully guide them out from the leaves; do this using a stake or

© CHARLES MARDEN FITCH

Ludisia discolor, one of several jewel orchids, is prized for its attractive foliage. In late winter and early spring, spires of white flowers top the rosettes of glossy leaves.

even a straw because it will not take much to adjust the spike's direction. When the inflorescence is about 10 to 12 inches tall, insert a permanent stake. Tie the spike to it loosely for directional guidance and support. This same tie can be gradually moved up the stake (to about 12 inches) as the spike lengthens. Always keep the string's point of contact with the spike at least 4 inches below the growing tip. Additional ties will likely be necessary as the spike elongates. Do not move the plant during the period of spike development; changing the plant's orientation to its light source will cause the spike to twist.

■ Position vandas to receive maximum available illumination; hang them above cattleyas.

DECEMBER

■ For those growing in a greenhouse or on the windowsill, pull back orchids whose leaves may be touching the inside of exterior glass or plastic surfaces to prevent damage to the leaves.

■ Do not allow the daytime temperatures to rise too high before ventilating the growing house after having it closed during the night or even during especially cold days. Fresh air is important for healthy plants.

■ Remove some, if not all, of the artificial shade on a glass or plastic greenhouse. Plants will continue to manufacture food during the winter, albeit at a reduced rate. Everything will occur at a slower pace until spring arrives.

■ *Cattleya skinneri* var. *alba* should be pushing its buds up into dried sheaths for a January flowering; do not cut the sheaths off or open. *Cattleya trianiae* and its hybrids ought to be blooming for several months beginning now. Many *Sophronitis* hybrids typically flower in this season. *Laelia anceps,* the Christmas orchid, will have well-defined buds just waiting for nature's signal to open.

■ The mule-ear oncidium, *Oncidium splendidum,* and the popular thin-leaved type, *Oncidium maculatum,* should be producing inflorescences. Stake the *Onc. splendidum* inflorescence as it grows upward, but do not allow the tip to droop as you would for a phalaenopsis.

■ Groom each *Phalaenopsis* spike. Use a fresh, clean stake. Avoid excess plant movement while the buds are developing or the buds may blast (wither). Be advised that high humidity in a closed house can also lead to flower spotting caused by *Botrytis*; provide supplementary air circulation using even a small fan just to avoid still air.

Amesiella philippinensis 'Newport Foam', HCC/AOS, is a good companion plant for phalaenopsis. Grower: Brian Hench.

■ *Ascocentrum aurantiacum* may have some inflorescences in flower by the end of the month; its beautiful yellow blooms are distinctive, although the plants resemble *Ascocentrum curvifolium* physically.

■ *Amesiella* (syn. *Angraceum*) *philippinensis* flowers in December, but some clones may bloom any time from now through March. Plants of *Tuberolabium kotoense* (called *Saccolabium quisumbingii* in the horticultural trade) are frequently confused with *Amesiella philippinensis,* but the flowers of the former are more numerous and are attractively speckled with rose to lavender spots. Both grow well in sphagnum moss, but *Amesiella philippinensis* prefers less light, similar to *Phalaenopsis*-like conditions.

■ *Nobile*-type dendrobiums may show some swollen nodes on their leafless pseudobulbs. By month's end, flowers can appear because the buds develop rapidly.

■ Some of the mottled-leaved *Paphiopedilum* species — *Paphiopedilum fairrieanum* and *Paphiopedilum sukhakulii* — bloom now. Keep their potting medium moist and avoid getting water in the pouch.

■ *Ludisia discolor* (syn. *Haemaria discolor*) will begin to develop inflorescences soon. Clean the foliage now, before the inflorescences grow, to maximize the beauty of the decorative foliage.

(Robert M. Scully Jr. is the former owner of Jones & Scully in Miami, Florida.)

Learning More

ORCHIDS ARE A PLEASURE TO GROW. Delight in the loveliness of your flowers will be multiplied when their beauty is shared with others. Join a local orchid society and the American Orchid Society to increase your appreciation of orchids.

Local Orchid Societies The American Orchid Society (AOS) has more than 550 Affiliated Societies worldwide. These are listed in the *AOS Orchid Source Directory*, which is sent free to all members of the Society, and this list is also posted on the Society's Web site, orchidweb.org.

American Orchid Society The AOS invites everyone interested in orchids to become a member of its growing ranks, which include beginners and experts alike. Founded in 1921, and with 30,000 members worldwide, the AOS is a nonprofit, scientific and horticultural organization that was established to extend the knowledge, production, use, perpetuation, preservation and appreciation of orchids.

As the preeminent orchid-related organization in the world today, the AOS accomplishes its nonprofit goals through financial support for important scientific research and wide-ranging conservation initiatives in orchids; through the collection and dissemination of information concerning the culture, hybridization or development of orchids by means of publications, lectures, films or otherwise; through maintenance of the orchid world's most comprehensive and prestigious awards system; and through many other avenues.

The AOS International Orchid Center in Delray Beach, Florida, is easily accessible from Interstate 95 and the Florida Turnpike. Members visiting the center will find educational presentations and programs; more than three-and-a-half acres of theme gardens, including a rainforest, Florida native habitat, formal garden, and the Lewis and Varina Vaughn Focus Garden (built in loving memory of the Society's greatest benefactors); orchid displays presented by local Affiliated Societies in the center's lobby; the Orchid Emporium gift shop and The AOS BookShop, with 200 orchid titles. Future plans for the new facility include a library and an auditorium for ongoing orchid education. AOS members are admitted free.

Primary among membership benefits is the Society's monthly, award-winning, 100-page magazine, *Orchids*. A new AOS member also receives a copy of *Your First Orchid*, which explains the basics of growing orchids. All members are given the *AOS Orchid Source Directory*, which includes a directory of commercial growers; access to a question and answer service; free admission to the AOS International Orchid Center in Delray Beach, Florida; and a 10 percent discount on educational materials purchased through The AOS BookShop and Orchid Emporium.

In addition, the Society maintains a progressive publications program that offers books, a calendar and two periodicals. *Lindleyana* is a quarterly scientific journal and *Awards Quarterly* presents photographs and detailed descriptions of each AOS-awarded flower and plant.

For information on joining the Society and visiting the International Orchid Center, please contact the Membership Services Department, American Orchid Society, 16700 AOS Lane, Delray Beach, Florida 33446-4351 (telephone 561-404-2000; e-mail TheAOS@ aos.org; Web site orchidweb.org).

AOS Judging Program Members of the American Orchid Society may apply to become orchid judges. Those selected must complete a rigorous training program of study, practical application, show attendance, and more. Information on this program is available from the International Orchid Center in Delray Beach. A list of Regional Judging Centers can be found in each issue of *Orchids*. The current edition of the *Handbook on Judging and Exhibition* is available from The AOS BookShop.

Suggested Reading

Orchid literature exists that covers all phases of orchids and orchid growing. Local libraries often have books about orchids, and many orchid societies have periodicals and references available to their members. Some county cooperative extension offices offer free brochures. An outstanding selection is available from The AOS BookShop. For a free booklist, call toll free 1-877-ORCHIDS (1-877-672-4437), or dial 561-404-2020.

Culture

All About Orchids, by Elvin McDonald. 1999 Revised Edition. Ortho Books, San Ramon, California. Softcover. 96 pages.

Growing Orchids Under Lights, by Charles Marden Fitch. 2002 Revised Edition. American Orchid Society, Delray Beach. Softcover. 76 pages.

Home Orchid Growing, by Rebecca T. Northen. 4th Edition. 1990. Prentice Hall Press, New York. Hardcover. 384 pages.

Orchid Pests and Diseases. 2002 Revised Edition. American Orchid Society, Delray Beach. Softcover. 118 pages.

You Can Grow Orchids, by Mary Noble. 5th Revised Edition. 1987. Published by author. Softcover. 128 pages.

Your First Orchid, by Stephen R. Batchelor. 2001 Revised Edition. American Orchid Society, Delray Beach. Softcover. 64 pages.

Identification

Golden Guide: Orchids, by F.S. Shuttleworth, H.S. Zim and G.W. Dillon; revised by Alec Pridgeon. 1997. Western Publishing, Racine. Softcover. 160 pages.

The Illustrated Encyclopedia of Orchids, edited by Alec Pridgeon. 1992. Timber Press, Portland. Hardcover. 304 pages.

The Manual of Cultivated Orchid Species, by Helmut Bechtel, Phillip Cribb and Edmund Launert. Third edition. 1992. The MIT Press, Cambridge. Hardcover. 528 pages.

Manual of Orchids, by Joyce Stewart. 1995. Timber Press, Portland. Hardcover. 388 pages.

BOB WANDS

Orchids are the star attraction at the Marie Selby Botanical Gardens in Sarasota, Florida, which features a superb collection.

Sources of Orchids

Orchids can be purchased at nurseries, plant sales and orchid shows. A listing of commercial growers is published in the *AOS Orchid Source Directory* and on the Society's Web site, orchidweb.org. Others can be found in the advertising section of *Orchids.*

Orchid Shows

Many local orchid societies hold annual orchid shows that range from small exhibits in shopping malls and banks to internationally famous expositions, such as those in New York, Miami, Santa Barbara and Japan. Orchid shows provide an excellent opportunity to view a variety of different species and hybrids, and purchase orchid plants of all sizes. A calendar in the monthly *Orchids* magazine lists orchid shows worldwide.

Public Orchid Collections

Botanical gardens and arboreta in the United States and abroad have public orchid collections, sometimes with a special theme. A comprehensive listing is printed in *The Orchid Tourist: An International Guide to Public Orchid Collections*, by Susan W. Plimpton, published by the American Orchid Society. This 64-page, softcover book arranges gardens by country and provides contact information as well as details on the size of the collection, main genera, and groups features and noteworthy aspects of the collection. Copies of this pocket-size guide are available from The AOS BookShop.

Special Interest Groups

Several special-interest groups print newsletters filled with detailed information and advertisements.

African Orchid Alliance, Patrick Denissen, 14 Speersstraat, 2020, Antwerp, Belgium (telephone and fax 323-2163406 [between 2 and 5 pm local time]; e-mail patrick.denissen@glo.be).

Catasetum/Stanhopea Alliance, Gordon Tingley, #1019-1450 Chestnut Street, Vancouver, BC, Canada V6J 3K3 (telephone 604-738-5010; to receive a free electronic newsletter, send your e-mail address to gtingley@interchange.ubc.ca).

Cymbidium Society of America, Inc., Matthew Swift, Membership Secretary, 6658 Carnelian Street, Rancho Cucamonga, California 91701-4515 (telephone 909-483-5590; fax 909-483-5590; e-mail cymsociety@prodigy.net; Web site www.cymbidium.org).

International Phalaenopsis Alliance, Kenneth Ross, MD, 7 Shearwater Court, Savannah, Georgia 31411-3030 (telephone 912-598-1282; fax 912-598-1336; e-mail kajr1@aol.com; Web site www.phal.org).

North American Native Orchid Alliance, Nancy A. Webb, 84 Etna Street, Brighton, Massachusetts 02135 (telephone 617-254-4815; Web site http://naorchid.org).

Odontoglossum Alliance, John Miller, PO Box 38, Westport Point, Massachusetts 02791 (telephone 508-636-8409; fax 508-636-6143; e-mail jemiller49@aol.com; Web site

http://www.odontoglossumalliance.org/).

The Orchid Badge Club International, Jack Woltmon, 1583 California Avenue, Wahiawa, Hawaii 96786 (telephone 808-622-1793; fax 808-622-4722; e-mail jwoltmon@aol.com).

Paphiopedilum Guild, Patty James, Treasurer, c/o The Orchid House, 1699 Sage, Los Osos, California 93402 (telephone 805-528-1417).

The Pleurothallid Alliance, 1721 Peavy Road, Howell, Michigan 48843 (e-mail freespirit@ismi.net; Web site http://members.ismi.net/pleurothallids/Pleurothallid_Alliance.htm).

Slipper Orchid Alliance, Richard Grundy, 950 Wikiup Drive, Santa Rosa, California 95403 (e-mail richard grundy@att.net).

The Virginia Paphiopedilum Society, Jerry Lawless, 3617 Matoaka Road, Hampton, Virginia 23661 (telephone 757-722-1850 [noon to 3 pm, or after 8 pm, ET]).

Identification of Orchid Species

The Orchid Identification Center (OIC) at the Marie Selby Botanical Gardens will identify orchid species for a nominal fee. For information and guidelines, contact the Orchid Identification Center, Marie Selby Botanical Gardens, 811 South Palm Avenue, Sarasota, Florida 34236 (telephone 941-955-7553; e-mail www.selby.org.contact.htm; Web site www.selby.org).

Orchids on the Internet

The AOS maintains *OrchidWeb*™, a massive site with articles, a calendar of orchid events, a Commercial Growers Directory, and more on the Internet at www.orchidweb.org. Surfing the Web will bring you to other sites of interest maintained by individuals and nurseries, among them: *Canadian Orchid Congress* (www.canadianorchidcongress.ca/), *Internet Orchid Species Photo Encyclopedia* (www.orchidspecies.com/), *OrchidMania* (www.orchids.org), *Orchids Australia* (www.infoweb.com.au/orchids/), and *The Orchid House* (http://retirees.uwaterloo.ca/~jerry/orchids/).

Glossary

aerial root A type of root produced above or away from the growing medium.

anther The part of the stamen containing the pollen; the tip of the column.

backbulb An old pseudobulb behind the actively growing portion of a sympodial orchid, often without leaves but still alive and bearing one or more dormant vegetative buds ("eyes").

bifoliate Having two leaves.

bigeneric Involving two distinct genera in the parentage; applied to hybrids.

cane An elongated dendrobium psuedo-bulb clothed with leaves.

chromosome One of the rod-like or bead-like bodies in the cell which contain the units of heredity called genes.

clone An individual plant raised from a single seed and all its subsequent vegetative propagations.

column The central organ of the orchid flower which contains both male (stamen) and female (pistil) parts; also called gynostegium and gynandrium.

crest A toothed, fringed or ridged adornment on the lip of some orchids.

crock Small pieces of broken earthenware or flower pots, placed in the bottom of a pot when repotting to aid in drainage.

cultivar An individual plant and its vegetative propagations in cultivation; a horticultural variety.

dorsal Pertaining to the back or the part turned away from the axis.

epiphyte A plant which naturally grows upon another plant but does not derive its nourishment from it; an "air plant."

fir bark A potting medium consisting of the chopped or ground bark of white fir, red fir or Douglas fir.

genus (pl. genera) A natural grouping of closely related but distinct species.

grex (pl. grexes) A hybrid progeny.

habit The characteristic form, aspect or mode of growth of a plant.

habitat The kind of locality in which a plant normally grows.

hybrid A cross between species or hybrids, the members of which frequently show characteristics of both parents.

inflorescence The flowering portion of a plant.

intergeneric hybrid A hybrid between members of two or more genera.

intrageneric hybrid A hybrid between species or hybrids within the same genus.

keiki The Hawaiian word for baby and applied to an offset or offshoot from an orchid plant.

lip A modified petal of the orchid flower, usually quite distinct from the other two petals; the labellum.

lithophyte Growing on a rock.

mericlone A propagule derived from tissue culture that is genetically identical to its parent.

monopodial A form of growth in which there is a single stem that continues to grow from its apex year after year.

Neotropics The New World Tropics.

nitrogen A major nutrient required by plants and indicated by the first of three numbers in a fertilizer formula.

Orchidaceae (or-kid-ACE-ee-ee) The orchid family.

osmunda/osmundine The cut fibrous roots of the osmunda fern used as a growing medium for orchids.

panicle An inflorescence with a main stem and branches, the flowers on the lower branches opening earlier than the upper ones.

petal One of the two inner segments of the orchid flower which is not modified as the lip.

phosphorus A major nutrient required by plants and indicated by the second of three numbers in a fertilizer formula.

pistil The ovule-bearing or seed-bearing organ of a flower, including, when complete, the ovary, style and stigma.

pollinium (pl. pollinia) The coherent mass of pollen grains found in the anther of orchids.

polyploid A term applied to a plant that possesses one or more extra sets of chromosomes beyond the normal diploid number.

potassium A major nutrient required by plants and indicated by the third number in a fertilizer formula.

pseudobulb A thickened portion of the stem of many orchids functioning in storage of water and nutrients.

quadrigeneric A hybrid genus with four genera in its background.

raceme An unbranched inflorescence of stalked flowers.

rhizome A root-bearing stem of sympodial orchids that progressively sends up leafy shoots.

scape An unbranched inflorescence with one flower.

sepal One of the three outer segments of the orchid flower.

sheath A modified leaf that encloses an emerging inflorescence or leaf.

species (singular and plural) A subdivision of a genus, and the fundamental unit of biological classification.

spike An unbranched inflorescence of unstalked flowers.

stamen The pollen-bearing organ of a flower, consisting of the filament and the anther.

stigma The part of the pistil that receives the pollen.

sympodial A form of growth in which each new shoot, springing from the rhizome of the previous growth, is complete in itself.

terrestrial Growing on the ground and supported by soil.

tree fern Tropical ferns, chiefly of the family Cyatheaceae, or the potting material made from cutting or shredding the trunk of such ferns; also known by the Hawaiian term hapu'u.

trigeneric Involving three distinct genera in the parentage; applied to hybrids.

unifoliate Having but one leaf.

velamen The thick layer of cells covering the roots of epiphytic orchids, which helps prevent water loss from internal tissues.

virus A type of infectious agent, much smaller than common microorganisms, several forms of which affect certain kinds of orchids.

Acknowledgments

Editor James B. Watson

Assistant Editors Susan Jones, Arlene Maguire

Production Assistant Jane Mengel

Contributing Editors Gary Baker, Ann and Phil Jesup

Proofreaders Lee S. Cooke, Mary Davidson Dunnell, Arnold Linsman, Sylvia M. Wood

Consulting Taxonomists Mark Chase, PhD (*Oncidium*), Eric Christenson, PhD ("Orchid Names"), Phillip Cribb, PhD (*Dendrobium*)

Index

Entries indexed include major subject headings and binomials in *italics*. Page numbers in **bold** indicate illustrations.

GROWING
Orchids
105

GROWING
Orchids

Cover Photographs